Super BIBLE ACTIVITIES 2 FOR KIDS

BARBOUR
PUBLISHING

Published by Barbour Publishing, Inc., P.O. Box 719, Uhrichsville, Ohio 44683, www.barbourbooks.com

Our mission is to publish and distribute inspirational products offering exceptional value and biblical encouragement to the masses.

Member of the
Evangelical Christian
Publishers Association

Printed in the United States of America.

INTRODUCTION

Hey, kids—

Looking for something to do on a rainy afternoon, a long car ride, or a night when there's nothing to watch on TV? Then you've come to the right place!

Super Bible Activities for Kids 2 is packed with nearly 150 fun puzzles. As you solve them, you'll be learning important truth from the Bible—and what could be better than that?

There are two sections in *Super Bible Activities for Kids 2*. Part 1 starts on the next page and offers 75 puzzles based on the Bible's book of Romans. Part 2 is all about grace, with another 73 puzzles. Answers for all the puzzles follow, beginning on page 339.

But enough of the talk. We know you're ready to begin, so jump on in. Enjoy!

COLOR *the* PICTURE

The Book of ROMANS

PAUL WROTE THE BOOK OF ROMANS FOR THE CHRISTIANS LIVING IN ROME.

THE PURPOSE FOR THIS LETTER WAS TO TEACH THAT NONE ARE PERFECT OR ABLE TO IMPRESS GOD. THERE IS ONLY ONE WHO IS PERFECT AND THAT IS JESUS CHRIST.

WHEN WE PUT OUR TRUST AND FAITH IN THE PERSON OF JESUS CHRIST, WE ARE FREE FROM THE POWER OF SIN. THROUGH JESUS' DEATH ON THE CROSS THE SIN ISSUE HAS BEEN SETTLED ONCE AND FOR ALL. THROUGH THE RESURRECTED LIFE OF CHRIST LIVING IN US, WE ARE GIVEN A NEW LIFE. WE ARE TOTALLY ACCEPTED AND LOVED BY GOD—NOT BY OUR OWN WORKS BUT BY THE WORK OF GOD'S SON, JESUS CHRIST.

DOUBLE *the* FUN

UNSCRAMBLE THE UNDERLINED WORDS IN EACH VERSE. ON THE NEXT PAGE, PLACE YOUR ANSWERS IN THE SPACES PROVIDED AND THEN COMPLETE THE CROSSWORD PUZZLE.

1. "PAUL, A SERVANT OF JESUS CHRIST, CALLED TO BE AN APOSTLE, SEPARATED UNTO THE LGEOPS OF GOD, (WHICH HE HAD PROMISED AFORE BY HIS STRPEOHP IN THE HOLY SCRIPTURES,) CONCERNING HIS SON JESUS CHRIST OUR LORD, WHICH WAS MADE OF THE SEED OF DAVID ACCORDING TO THE FLESH."

ROMANS 1:1–3, KJV

2. "AND DECLARED TO BE THE SON OF GOD WITH RPEWO, ACCORDING TO THE TSIPIR OF HOLINESS, BY THE RESURRECTION FROM THE DEAD."

ROMANS 1:4, KJV

3. "EGCRA TO YOU AND PEACE FROM GOD OUR RFEAHT, AND THE LORD JESUS TCHSIR."

ROMANS 1:7, KJV

1. _____ _____

2. _____ _____

3. _____ _____

_____

FINISH *the* VERSE

USE THE CODE CHART BELOW TO FINISH THE
VERSE ON THE NEXT PAGE. (EXAMPLE: K=24)

	1	2	3	4	5	6	7
1	A	B	C	D	E	F	G
2	H	I	J	K	L	M	N
3	O	P	Q	R	S	T	U
4	V	W	X	Y	Z		

"I AM NOT __ __ __ __ __ __ __
          11 35 21 11 26 15 14

OF   THE   __ __ __ __ __ __,
           17 31 35 32 15 25

BECAUSE   IT   IS   THE

__ __ __ __ __   OF   __ __ __   FOR
32 31 42 15 34   17 31 14

THE   __ __ __ __ __ __ __ __ __
      35 11 25 41 11 36 22 31 27

OF __ __ __ __ __ __ __ __   WHO
   15 41 15 34 44 31 27 15

BELIEVES: FIRST FOR THE __ __ __,
                        23 15 42

THEN FOR THE __ __ __ __ __ __ __."
             17 15 27 36 22 25 15

ROMANS 1:16

11

SCRAMBLED VERSES

UNSCRAMBLE THE WORDS BELOW AND COMPLETE THE VERSE ON THE NEXT PAGE.

"EHT HWART FO DGO SI GIBEN ERLVAEDE MFOR NHEEVA GAAISTN LAL EHT DGOSLESSNES DNA SWCIKDEENS FO NME OHW SPUSSERP EHT THTUR YB RTIHE SWCIKDEENS, ECNIS THWA YMA EB NKWON TBAUO DGO SI NLPIA OT MTEH, EBACUSE DGO SHA EMDA TI NLPIA OT MTEH."

"___ __ __ ____ __
__ __ __ _____
_____ ____
_____ _____
___ ___ _____-
____ ____ _____-
____ __ ___
___ _____
___ _____ __
____ _____-
____, _____ ____
___ __ ____
____ ___ __
____ __ ____,
_____ ___ ___
____ __ ____
__ ____."

ROMANS 1:18–19

13

WORD SEARCH

FIND THE WORDS LISTED BELOW IN THE WORD SEARCH ON THE NEXT PAGE.

GRACE   PEACE   FATHER   POWER   WORKS   GENTILE   CHRIST   PERFECT   JEW   PROPHETS   SPIRIT

```
H R Q L F A T H E R F D
F J G O N C L M F K C W
G S J V P O W E R A A B
R D S E B D F E R R K L
A N P P E L W G G O R R
C P I R B W O R K S O D
E Z R E B V C X U R S T
W A I T R B C H R I S T
H A T P I N T M E J E W
Q L R V B C T S S D C L
M W I B E P D P E A C E
B Y D F B C E K C H L Q
T C R P A G E N T I L E
N E J E B G E N T E N W
P R O P H E T S Q I O P
```

FILL *in the* BLANKS

USING THE WORDS BELOW, COMPLETE THE
VERSE ON THE NEXT PAGE.

KNOWING   CREATED
EARTH   POWER
INVISIBLE   WORLD
GOD   CLEARLY
EXCUSE   NATURE

"FOR EVER SINCE THE _____ WAS _____,
PEOPLE HAVE SEEN THE _____ AND SKY.
THROUGH EVERYTHING ___ MADE, THEY CAN
_____ SEE HIS _____ QUALITIES—HIS
ETERNAL _____ AND DIVINE _____. SO THEY
HAVE NO _____ FOR NOT _____ GOD."

ROMANS 1:20, NLT

17

CROSSWORD

ROMANS 1:21–23

ACROSS

1. "FOR ALTHOUGH THEY KNEW _____."
2. "THEY NEITHER _____ HIM AS GOD NOR GAVE THANKS TO HIM."
3. "BUT THEIR THINKING BECAME _____."
4. "AND THEIR FOOLISH _____ WERE DARKENED."

DOWN

1. "ALTHOUGH THEY _____ TO BE WISE."
2. "THEY _____ FOOLS."
3. "AND EXCHANGED THE _____ OF THE IMMORTAL GOD."
4. "FOR IMAGES MADE TO LOOK LIKE MORTAL MAN AND BIRDS AND _____ AND REPTILES."

19

COLOR *the* PICTURE

"FOR THEREIN IS THE RIGHTEOUSNESS OF GOD REVEALED FROM FAITH TO FAITH: AS IT IS WRITTEN, THE JUST SHALL LIVE BY FAITH."

ROMANS 1:17, KJV

SCRAMBLED VERSES

UNSCRAMBLE THE WORDS BELOW AND COMPLETE THE VERSE ON THE NEXT PAGE.

"UYO, TEHROEFRE, EHVA ON XESCEU, UYO WOH SPSA TJNUEDMG NO ESNOOME ESLE, RFO TA RWHETAVE TPNIO UYO EJUGD EHT RTOHE, UYO EAR GCNONIDMEN FYUOLESR, EBEACUS UYO OWH SPAS TJUNDEGM OD EHT EMSA STIHNG."

22

"___ ___, ___ ___ ___ ___ ___ ___ ___ ___,
___ ___ ___ ___ ___ ___ ___ ___ ___,
___ ___ ___ ___ ___ ___ ___ ___ ___
___ ___ ___ ___ ___ ___ ___ ___
___ ___ ___ ___ ___ ___ ___ ___ ___,
___ ___ ___ ___ ___ ___ ___ ___ ___ ___
___ ___ ___ ___ ___ ___ ___ ___ ___
___ ___ ___ ___ ___ ___ ___, ___ ___ ___
___ ___ ___ ___ ___ ___ ___ ___ ___
___ ___ ___ ___ ___ ___ ___, ___ ___-
___ ___ ___ ___ ___ ___ ___ ___
___ ___ ___ ___ ___ ___ ___ ___-
___ ___ ___ ___ ___ ___ ___ ___ ___
___ ___ ___ ___ ___ ___ ___ ___ ___."

ROMANS 2:1

FILL *in the* BLANKS

USING THE WORDS BELOW, COMPLETE THE
VERSES ON THE NEXT PAGE.

MEANT	JUDGMENT
KNOWING	YOURSELF
REPENTANCE	SUPPOSE
PRESUME	JUDGE
KINDNESS	RICHES
ESCAPE	GOD'S
PRACTICE	

"DO YOU _____, O MAN—YOU WHO _____
THOSE WHO _____ SUCH THINGS AND
YET DO THEM _____—THAT YOU WILL
_____ THE _____ OF GOD? OR DO YOU
_____ ON THE _____ OF HIS _____
AND FORBEARANCE AND PATIENCE, NOT
_____ THAT ___'_ KINDNESS IS _____ TO
LEAD YOU TO _____?"

ROMANS 2:3–4, ESV

25

FINISH *the* VERSE

USE THE CODE CHART BELOW TO FINISH THE
VERSES ON THE NEXT PAGE. (EXAMPLE: K=24)

	1	2	3	4	5	6	7
1	A	B	C	D	E	F	G
2	H	I	J	K	L	M	N
3	O	P	Q	R	S	T	U
4	V	W	X	Y	Z		

"NOW __ __ __, IF YOU CALL
44 31 37

__ __ __ __ __ __ __ __ A JEW;
44 31 37 34 35 15 25 16

IF YOU __ __ __ __ ON THE LAW
34 15 25 44

AND __ __ __ __ ABOUT YOUR
12 34 11 17

__ __ __ __ __ __ __ __ __ __ __ TO
34 15 25 11 36 22 31 27 35 21 22 32

__ __ __ ; IF YOU KNOW HIS __ __ __ __
17 31 14   42 22 25 25

AND __ __ __ __ __ __ OF WHAT IS
11 32 32 34 31 41 15

__ __ __ __ __ __ __ __ BECAUSE YOU
35 37 32 15 34 22 31 34

ARE __ __ __ __ __ __ __ __ __ __ BY
22 27 35 36 34 37 13 36 15 14

THE LAW."

ROMANS 2:17–18

27

DOUBLE *the* FUN

UNSCRAMBLE THE UNDERLINED WORDS IN EACH VERSE. ON THE NEXT PAGE, PLACE YOUR ANSWERS IN THE SPACES PROVIDED AND THEN COMPLETE THE CROSSWORD PUZZLE.

1. "IF YOU ARE <u>DCOENCVIN</u> THAT YOU ARE A GUIDE FOR THE <u>DBNLI</u>, A <u>TLHIG</u> FOR THOSE WHO ARE IN THE DARK."

ROMANS 2:19

2. "AN <u>RIOTNSTCRU</u> OF THE <u>LOFOSIH</u>, TEACHER OF INFANTS, BECAUSE YOU HAVE IN THE <u>WLA</u> THE EMBODIMENT OF KNOWLEDGE AND <u>TTHUR</u>."

ROMANS 2:20

3. "YOU, THEN, WHO <u>CHTAE</u> OTHERS, DO YOU NOT TEACH YOURSELF?"

ROMANS 2:21

1. _____ _____
   _____

2. _____ _____
   _____ _____

3. _____

SCRAMBLED VERSES

UNSCRAMBLE THE WORDS BELOW AND COMPLETE THE VERSES ON THE NEXT PAGE.

"ETEHR SI ON ENO SRUIGOHET, TNO VENE ENO; ETHRE SI ON EON WOH SUDNDAERTNS, ON EON OHW SSKEE DGO. LAL EHVA DTEUNR YWAA, YHTE VAHE RTOEGEHT EBMECO SWSOERLHT; ETREH SI ON ENO OHW EDSO DGOO, TON NEVE EON."

"__ __ __ __ __ __ __ __
__ __ __ __ __ __ __ __ __,
__ __ __ __ __ __ __;
__ __ __ __ __ __
__ __ __ __ __ __ __ -
__ __ __ __ __, __ __ __ __
__ __ __ __ __ __ __.
__ __ __ __ __ __
__ __ __, __ __ __ __
__ __ __ __ __ __ __
__ __ __ __ __; __ __ __
__ __ __ __ __ __ __
__ __ __ __ __, __ __
__ __ __ __ __."

ROMANS 3:10–12

31

DOUBLE *the* FUN

UNSCRAMBLE THE UNDERLINED WORDS IN EACH VERSE. ON THE NEXT PAGE, PLACE YOUR ANSWERS IN THE SPACES PROVIDED AND THEN COMPLETE THE CROSSWORD PUZZLE.

1. "ALL HAVE <u>DTEUNR</u> AWAY, THEY HAVE TOGETHER BECOME <u>SWSOERLTH</u>;

ROMANS 3:12

2. "THERE IS NO <u>ENO</u> WHO DOES <u>DOGO</u>, NOT EVEN ONE."

ROMANS 3:12

3. "THEIR <u>TSTHARO</u> ARE OPEN GRAVES; THEIR TONGUES PRACTICE <u>TDIECE</u>. THE POISON OF <u>SVRIEP</u> IS ON THEIR <u>SLPI</u>."

ROMANS 3:13

1. _____ _____

2. _____ _____

3. _____ _____

_____ _____

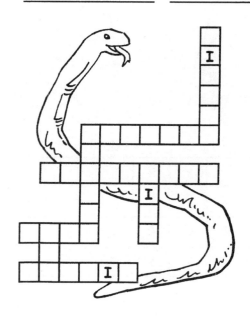

FINISH *the* VERSE

USE THE CODE CHART BELOW TO FINISH THE
VERSES ON THE NEXT PAGE. (EXAMPLE: K=24)

	1	2	3	4	5	6	7
1	A	B	C	D	E	F	G
2	H	I	J	K	L	M	N
3	O	P	Q	R	S	T	U
4	V	W	X	Y	Z		

"THEIR __ __ __ __ __ __ ARE
26 31 37 36 21 35

FULL OF __ __ __ __ __ __ __
13 37 34 35 22 27 17

AND BITTERNESS. THEIR FEET

ARE __ __ __ __ __ TO SHED
35 42 22 16 36

__ __ __ __ __; RUIN AND
12 25 31 31 14

__ __ __ __ __ __ MARK THEIR
26 22 35 15 34 44

WAYS, AND THE WAY OF

__ __ __ __ __ THEY DO NOT
32 15 11 13 15

KNOW."

ROMANS 3:14–17

35

WORD SEARCH

FIND THE WORDS UNDERLINED BELOW IN THE WORD SEARCH ON THE NEXT PAGE.

"BUT NOW THE <u>RIGHTEOUSNESS</u> OF GOD WITHOUT THE <u>LAW</u> IS <u>MANIFESTED</u>, BEING WITNESSED BY THE LAW AND THE <u>PROPHETS</u>; EVEN THE RIGHTEOUSNESS OF <u>GOD</u> WHICH IS BY <u>FAITH</u> OF <u>JESUS</u> CHRIST UNTO ALL AND UPON ALL THEM THAT <u>BELIEVE</u>."

ROMANS 3:21–22, KJV

```
R R W B E L I E V E O B
F I Y D C E O U R E W L
T G G N P R O P H E T S
R H R E P R L G S R D K
K T C P Y E O X T R D N
H E Q O N T F U S E S B
F O G O B K E S T N T W
G U J V O L U S I L Y N
S S B E R B E L S A N T
P N T O U F D E B W I I
T E L H I B E J E S U S
R S T N I N D G O D N N
W S A T B S H I N B O V
H M P P B P T N Q S L N
Q F A I T H H N U H W V
```

SECRET CODES

TO SOLVE THE CODED VERSES BELOW, LOOK
AT EACH LETTER AND WRITE THE ONE THAT
COMES BEFORE IT IN THE ALPHABET.

"GPS BMM IBWF TJOOFE BOE GBMM
TIPSU PG UIF HMPSZ PG HPE, BOE BSF
KVTUJGJFE GSFFMZ CZ IJT HSBDF
UISPVHI UIF SFEFNQUJPO UIBU DBNF
CZ DISJTU KFTVT."

A B C D E F G H I J K L M N O P Q R S T
U V W X Y Z

"___ ___ ____
_____ ___ ____
_____ __ ____
_____ __ ____,
___ ___ _____-
_____ _____
__ ___ _____
_____ ___
_____ ____
____ __ _____
_____."

ROMANS 3:23–24

39

CROSSWORD

ROMANS 3:25–26

<u>**ACROSS**</u>

1. "GOD PRESENTED HIM AS A SACRIFICE OF
   _____."

2. "THROUGH _____ IN HIS BLOOD."

3. "HE DID THIS TO DEMONSTRATE HIS
   _____"

4. "BECAUSE IN HIS FORBEARANCE HE HAD
   LEFT THE SINS _____ BEFOREHAND
   UNPUNISHED."

<u>**DOWN**</u>

1. "HE DID IT TO _____ HIS
   JUSTICE AT THE PRESENT TIME."

2. "SO AS TO BE _____."

3. "AND THE _____ WHO JUSTIFIES."

4. "THOSE WHO HAVE FAITH IN _____."

41

FILL *in the* BLANKS

USING THE WORDS BELOW, COMPLETE THE
VERSES ON THE NEXT PAGE.

GENTILES	JUSTIFIED
GOD	WORKS
MAN	DEEDS
FAITH	BOASTING
LAW	JEWS

"WHERE IS _____ THEN? IT IS EXCLUDED. BY WHAT _____? OF _____? NAY: BUT BY THE LAW OF _____. THEREFORE WE CONCLUDE THAT A _____ IS _____ BY FAITH WITHOUT THE _____ OF THE LAW. IS HE THE _____ OF THE _____ ONLY? IS HE NOT ALSO OF THE GENTILES? YES, OF THE _____ ALSO."

ROMANS 3:27–29, KJV

COLOR *the* PICTURE

"SAYING, BLESSED ARE THEY WHOSE INIQUITIES ARE FORGIVEN, AND WHOSE SINS ARE COVERED. BLESSED IS THE MAN TO WHOM THE LORD WILL NOT IMPUTE SIN."

ROMANS 4:7–8, KJV

FINISH *the* VERSE

USE THE CODE CHART BELOW TO FINISH THE
VERSES ON THE NEXT PAGE. (EXAMPLE: K=24)

	1	2	3	4	5	6	7
1	A	B	C	D	E	F	G
2	H	I	J	K	L	M	N
3	O	P	Q	R	S	T	U
4	V	W	X	Y	Z		

"THEREFORE, SINCE WE HAVE BEEN __ __ __ __ __ __ __ __ __
23 37 35 36 22 16 22 15 14

THROUGH __ __ __ __ __ , WE
16 11 22 36 21

HAVE __ __ __ __ __ WITH GOD
32 15 11 13 15

THROUGH OUR __ __ __ __ JESUS
25 31 34 14

CHRIST, THROUGH WHOM WE HAVE GAINED ACCESS BY FAITH INTO THIS __ __ __ __ __ IN
17 34 11 13 15

WHICH WE NOW __ __ __ __ __."
35 36 11 27 14

ROMANS 5:1–2

47

SCRAMBLED VERSES

UNSCRAMBLE THE WORDS BELOW AND COMPLETE THE VERSES ON THE NEXT PAGE.

"TON YNLO OS, TUB EW OSLA ERECJOI NI URO SFUSFGENRI, EBSECUA EW WKON TAHT FUSFGENRI SPORUDEC EPCENRSAERVE; EPCENRSAERVE, CRHEATRCA; DAN TACARHCER, EPOH."

48

"— — —   — — — —   — —,
— — —   — —   — — — —
— — — — — — —   — —
— — —   — — — — — — — —,
— — — — — —   — —   — — —
— — — —   — — — — — —
— — — — — — — — — —
— — — — — — — — — ;
— — — — — — — — — — —,
— — — — — — — ;   — — —
— — — — — — — —   —,
— — — —."

ROMANS 5:3–4

49

WORD SEARCH

FIND THE WORDS UNDERLINED BELOW IN THE WORD SEARCH ON THE NEXT PAGE.

"AND <u>HOPE</u> MAKETH NOT <u>ASHAMED</u>; BECAUSE THE <u>LOVE</u> OF <u>GOD</u> IS SHED <u>ABROAD</u> IN OUR <u>HEARTS</u> BY THE <u>HOLY</u> <u>GHOST</u> WHICH IS <u>GIVEN</u> UNTO US."

ROMANS 5:5, KJV

```
V S H B E O B R S S I S
L H O P E R M P D H P T
W T Z O H U B I G O D Y
T R A T P B N D M S D D
E W A C T E S N S B F I
R H D P P B P D Z C H L
H O L Y V A B R O A D A
K S W I B B T T I N B S
F G Y D L O V E N P S H
T H O N C E I N T U H A
O O H E R S E D E K O M
K S C P D V D T L E U E
H T Q O I C L G E W L D
F S G G N T B X S R D D
G D J V H E A R T S T A
```

FILL *in the* BLANKS

USING THE WORDS BELOW, COMPLETE THE
VERSES ON THE NEXT PAGE.

DARE   DIED
RIGHTEOUS STRENGTH
UNGODLY   TIME
WHEN   GOOD

"FOR ____ WE WERE YET WITHOUT _____,
IN DUE ____ CHRIST ____ FOR THE _____.
FOR SCARCELY FOR A _____ MAN WILL
ONE DIE: YET PERADVENTURE FOR A ____ MAN
SOME WOULD EVEN ____ TO DIE."

ROMANS 5:6-7, KJV

SECRET CODES

TO SOLVE THE CODED VERSE BELOW, LOOK
AT EACH LETTER AND WRITE THE ONE THAT
COMES BEFORE IT IN THE ALPHABET.

"CVU HPE EFNPOTUSBUFT IJT PXO
MPWF GPS VT JO UIJT: XIJMF XF
XFSF TUJMM TJOOFST, DISJTU EJFE
GPS VT."

A B C D E F G H I J K L M N O P Q R S T
U V W X Y Z

"___ ___ _____-
_____ ___ ___ ___
____ ___ __ __
____: _____ __
____ _____
_____, _____
____ ___ __."

ROMANS 5:8

FILL *in the* BLANKS

USING THE WORDS BELOW, COMPLETE THE
VERSES ON THE NEXT PAGE.

SON
CONDEMNATION
SAVE
MADE
ENEMIES

FRIENDSHIP
CHRIST
DEATH
SIGHT
LIFE

"AND SINCE WE HAVE BEEN _____ RIGHT IN GOD'S _____ BY THE BLOOD OF _____, HE WILL CERTAINLY _____ US FROM GOD'S _____. FOR SINCE OUR _____ WITH GOD WAS RESTORED BY THE _____ OF HIS SON WHILE WE WERE STILL HIS _____, WE WILL CERTAINLY BE SAVED THROUGH THE _____ OF HIS _____."

ROMANS 5:9–10, NLT

COLOR *the* PICTURE

"FOR IF, WHEN WE WERE ENEMIES, WE WERE RECONCILED TO GOD BY THE DEATH OF HIS SON, MUCH MORE, BEING RECONCILED, WE SHALL BE SAVED BY HIS LIFE."

ROMANS 5:10, KJV

FINISH *the* VERSE

USE THE CODE CHART BELOW TO FINISH THE
VERSES ON THE NEXT PAGE. (EXAMPLE: K=24)

	1	2	3	4	5	6	7
1	A	B	C	D	E	F	G
2	H	I	J	K	L	M	N
3	O	P	Q	R	S	T	U
4	V	W	X	Y	Z		

"THEREFORE, JUST AS __ __ __
                     35 22 27

ENTERED   THE   __ __ __ __ __
                42 31 34 25 14

THROUGH ONE __ __ __, AND
              26 11 27

__ __ __ __ __ THROUGH __ __ __,
14 15 11 36 21   35 22 27

AND IN THIS WAY DEATH CAME TO

__ __ __   MEN,   BECAUSE   ALL
11 25 25

__ __ __ __ __ __ —FOR BEFORE THE
35 22 27 27 15 14

__ __ __ WAS GIVEN, SIN WAS IN
25 11 42

THE __ __ __ __ __."
    42 31 34 25 14

ROMANS 5:12–13

61

DOUBLE *the* FUN

UNSCRAMBLE THE UNDERLINED WORDS IN
EACH VERSE. ON THE NEXT PAGE, PLACE YOUR
ANSWERS IN THE SPACES PROVIDED AND
THEN COMPLETE THE CROSSWORD PUZZLE.

1. "BUT THE GIFT IS NOT LIKE THE
STSRAESP. FOR IF THE MANY IDED BY THE
TRESPASS OF THE ONE MAN. . ."

ROMANS 5:15

2. "HOW MUCH MORE DID SGDO ECRAG AND
THE GIFT THAT EMAC BY GRACE OF ONE
MAN."

ROMANS 5:15

3. "JESUS SCTIRH, OWVOELFR TO THE
MANY!"

ROMANS 5:15

1. _____   _____

2. _____   _____

   _____

3. _____   _____

WORD SEARCH

FIND THE WORDS UNDERLINED BELOW IN THE WORD SEARCH ON THE NEXT PAGE.

"AGAIN, THE <u>GIFT</u> OF <u>GOD</u> IS NOT LIKE THE <u>RESULT</u> OF THE ONE MAN'S <u>SIN</u>: THE <u>JUDGMENT</u> FOLLOWED ONE SIN AND BROUGHT <u>CONDEMNATION</u>, BUT THE GIFT FOLLOWED MANY <u>TRESPASSES</u> AND BROUGHT <u>JUSTIFICATION</u>."

ROMANS 5:16

```
J U Y R I Y I U D E S C
U T C O J M V D T E E O
S O R D P D C L S E W N
T K K C O Y T S X S R D
I H R Q O N A F L T R E
F F J G V P L E D H P M
I G S J S O B O D S I N
C S D E O R G I L I T A
A P R T H U B D M S D T
T T P L F G I F T B F I
I R Z T T I S D Z C H O
O W R E S U L T K T K N
N H A P V B C T I N B N
J U D G M E N T B Q S O
K M W I B A I T T U C L
```

65

CROSSWORD

ROMANS 5:17–18

ACROSS

1. "FOR IF, BY THE _____ OF THE ONE MAN. . ."
2. "_____ REIGNED THROUGH THAT ONE MAN."
3. "HOW MUCH MORE WILL THOSE WHO _____."
4. "GOD'S ABUNDANT PROVISION OF _____."

DOWN

1. "AND OF THE GIFT OF _____."
2. "REIGN IN LIFE THROUGH THE ONE MAN, _____ CHRIST."
3. "CONSEQUENTLY, JUST AS THE RESULT OF ONE TRESPASS WAS CONDEMNATION FOR ALL _____."
4. "SO ALSO THE RESULT OF ONE _____ OF RIGHTEOUSNESS WAS JUSTIFICATION THAT BRINGS LIFE FOR ALL MEN."

FINISH *the* VERSE

USE THE CODE CHART BELOW TO FINISH THE
VERSE ON THE NEXT PAGE. (EXAMPLE: K=24)

	1	2	3	4	5	6	7
1	A	B	C	D	E	F	G
2	H	I	J	K	L	M	N
3	O	P	Q	R	S	T	U
4	V	W	X	Y	Z		

"FOR JUST AS THROUGH THE

___ ___ ___ ___ ___ ___ ___ ___ ___ ___ ___
14 22 35 31 12 15 14 22 15 27 13 15

OF THE ONE MAN THE MANY WERE

MADE ___ ___ ___ ___ ___ ___ ___, SO
     35 22 27 27 15 34 35

ALSO   THROUGH   THE

___ ___ ___ ___ ___ ___ ___ ___ ___
31 12 15 14 22 15 27 13 15

OF   THE   ONE ___ ___ ___ THE
                      26 11 27

___ ___ ___ ___ WILL   BE   MADE
26 11 27 44

                              "
___ ___ ___ ___ ___ ___ ___ ___ ___.
34 22 17 21 36 15 31 37 35

ROMANS 5:19

69

SCRAMBLED VERSES

UNSCRAMBLE THE WORDS BELOW AND COMPLETE THE VERSES ON THE NEXT PAGE.

"TWHA LSLHA EW YSA, NTHE? LSLHA

EW OG NO GSNIINN OS TAHT EGARC

YMA EISNACER? YB ON SMNEA! EW

IDED OT NSI; WHO NCA EW ELVI NI

TI YNA RLEONG?"

"— ——— — ————— — ——
———, ————_? ————— —
—— —— —— ————— ——
— — ———— ————— —
——— ————————_?
— — — — ————_!
—— ———— —— ——_;
——— ——— —— ————
— — — — — — —
—————_?"

ROMANS 6:1–2

FILL *in the* BLANKS

USING THE WORDS BELOW, COMPLETE THE
VERSES ON THE NEXT PAGE.

LIFE	DEATH
RAISED	BAPTIZED
BURIED	KNOW
GLORY	ORDER
JESUS	WALK

"DO YOU NOT _____ THAT ALL OF US WHO HAVE BEEN _____ INTO CHRIST _____ WERE BAPTIZED INTO HIS _____? WE WERE _____ THEREFORE WITH HIM BY BAPTISM INTO DEATH, IN _____ THAT, JUST AS CHRIST WAS _____ FROM THE DEAD BY THE _____ OF THE FATHER, WE TOO MIGHT ____ IN NEWNESS OF ____."

ROMANS 6:3–4, ESV

DOUBLE *the* FUN

UNSCRAMBLE THE UNDERLINED WORDS IN
EACH VERSE. ON THE NEXT PAGE, PLACE YOUR
ANSWERS IN THE SPACES PROVIDED AND
THEN COMPLETE THE CROSSWORD PUZZLE.

1. "IF WE HAVE BEEN <u>DUNETI</u> WITH HIM
LIKE THIS IN HIS <u>HDTEA</u>, WE WILL
CERTAINLY ALSO BE UNITED WITH <u>IMH</u> IN
HIS RESURRECTION."

ROMANS 6:5

2. "FOR WE KNOW THAT OUR OLD SELF WAS
<u>CDREUICFI</u> WITH HIM SO THAT THE BODY OF
SIN <u>GTHMI</u> BE DONE AWAY WITH."

ROMANS 6:6

3. "THAT WE SHOULD NO LONGER BE SLAVES
TO SIN—BECAUSE ANYONE WHO HAS <u>DDIE</u>
HAS BEEN <u>EFERD</u> FROM SIN."

ROMANS 6:6–7

1. _____ _____

_____

2. _____ _____

3. _____ _____

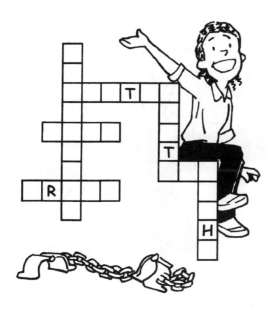

FILL *in the* BLANKS

USING THE WORDS BELOW, COMPLETE THE VERSES ON THE NEXT PAGE.

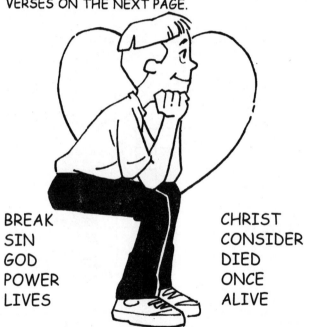

BREAK
SIN
GOD
POWER
LIVES

CHRIST
CONSIDER
DIED
ONCE
ALIVE

"WHEN HE ____, HE DIED ____ TO ____ THE ____ OF SIN. BUT NOW THAT HE ____, HE LIVES FOR THE GLORY OF ___. SO YOU ALSO SHOULD _____ YOURSELVES TO BE DEAD TO THE POWER OF ___ AND ____ TO GOD THROUGH ____ JESUS."

ROMANS 6:10–11, NLT

SECRET CODES

TO SOLVE THE CODED VERSE BELOW, LOOK AT EACH LETTER AND WRITE THE ONE THAT COMES BEFORE IT IN THE ALPHABET.

"GPS TJO TIBMM OPU CF ZPVS

NBTUFS, CFDBVTF ZPV BSF OPU

VOEFS MBX, CVU VOEFS HSBDF."

78

A B C D E F G H I J K L M N O P Q R S T
U V W X Y Z

"— —— — —— ———— —

——— —— ————

—————, ———————

——— ——— ———

————— ———, ———

————— —————."

ROMANS 6:14

79

SCRAMBLED VERSES

UNSCRAMBLE THE WORDS BELOW AND COMPLETE THE VERSE ON THE NEXT PAGE.

"OS, YM SBRREOHT, UYO OASL DIDE OT HTE WLA THGHUOR ETH YBDO FO TCSHIR, THTA UYO TGMHI GBELNO OT RANEHTO, OT MIH OHW SWA DREASI MFRO HET DADE, NI DRROE HTTA EW TMGIH RBAE TFIUR OT DGO."

"__ __, __ __ _____,
___ ____ ____ __
___ ___ _____
__ __ __ ____ __
_____, ____ ___
____ _____ __
_____, __ ___
___ ___ _____
___ ___ _____,
__ _____ ____
__ _____ ____
____ __ ___."

ROMANS 7:4

CROSSWORD

ROMANS 7:6, 7:21–22

ACROSS

1. "BUT NOW, BY DYING TO WHAT ONCE _____ US."
2. "WE HAVE BEEN RELEASED FROM THE _____."
3. "SO THAT WE SERVE IN THE NEW WAY OF THE _____."
4. "AND NOT IN THE _____ WAY OF THE WRITTEN CODE."

DOWN

1. "SO I FIND THIS LAW AT _____."
2. "WHEN I WANT TO DO _____."
3. "_____ IS RIGHT THERE WITH ME."
4. "FOR IN MY INNER BEING I _____ IN GOD'S LAW."

WORD SEARCH

FIND THE WORDS UNDERLINED BELOW IN THE WORD SEARCH ON THE NEXT PAGE.

"THERE IS THEREFORE NOW NO <u>CONDEMNATION</u> TO <u>THEM</u> WHICH ARE IN <u>CHRIST</u> JESUS, WHO WALK NOT AFTER THE FLESH, BUT AFTER THE SPIRIT. FOR THE <u>LAW</u> OF THE <u>SPIRIT</u> OF <u>LIFE</u> IN CHRIST <u>JESUS</u> HATH MADE ME <u>FREE</u> FROM THE LAW OF <u>SIN</u> AND <u>DEATH</u>."

ROMANS 8:1–2, KJV

```
L M W I F R E E I Q S L
A B Y D B A Q N N U H W
W C T H E M E T T K O C
O T H E R T T D E E U O
K K C P S F R A E W L N
H R Q I Y C L G N R D D
F J R O N T B I S R T E
G H J V B K S L T I S M
C D B E O L E S S P T N
P E T O S P I R I T Y A
T P L H U M I L I D N T
R Z J E S U S M L F I I
W A C T I N E S I H L O
D E A T H S D Z F K N N
Q L R V B P H K E B O R
```

85

SECRET CODES

TO SOLVE THE CODED VERSE BELOW, LOOK AT EACH LETTER AND WRITE THE ONE THAT COMES BEFORE IT IN THE ALPHABET.

"GPS XIBU UIF MBX XBT QPXFSMFTT

UP EP JO UIBU JU XBT XFBLFOFE CZ

UIF TJOGVM OBUVSF, HPE EJE CZ

TFOEJOH IJT PXO TPO JO UIF

MJLFOFTT PG TJOGVM NBO UP CF B

TJO PGGFSJOH."

A B C D E F G H I J K L M N O P Q R S T
U V W X Y Z

"___ ____ ___
___ ___ _____-
____ __ __
____ __ ___
_____ __
___ _____
_____', ___
___ __ _____
___ ___ ___ __
___ _____
__ _____ ____
__ __ __ __ ___
_____."

ROMANS 8:3

87

FILL *in the* BLANKS

USING THE WORDS BELOW, COMPLETE THE VERSE ON THE NEXT PAGE.

SPIRIT   LAW
MIGHT   WEAK
WALK   SON
FLESH   CONDEMNED
GOD   RIGHTEOUSNESS

"FOR WHAT THE ___ COULD NOT DO, IN THAT IT WAS ___ THROUGH THE FLESH, ___ SENDING HIS OWN ___ IN THE LIKENESS OF SINFUL ___, AND FOR SIN, ___ SIN IN THE FLESH: THAT THE ___ OF THE LAW ___ BE FULFILLED IN US, WHO ___ NOT AFTER THE FLESH, BUT AFTER THE ___."

ROMANS 8:3–4, KJV

FINISH *the* VERSE

USE THE CODE CHART BELOW TO FINISH THE
VERSE ON THE NEXT PAGE. (EXAMPLE: K=24)

	1	2	3	4	5	6	7
1	A	B	C	D	E	F	G
2	H	I	J	K	L	M	N
3	O	P	Q	R	S	T	U
4	V	W	X	Y	Z		

"THOSE WHO LIVE

__ __ __ __ __ __ __ __ __
11 13 13 31 34 14 22 27 17

TO THE __ __ __ __ __ __
35 22 27 16 37 25

__ __ __ __ __ __ HAVE THEIR
27 11 36 37 34 15

__ __ __ __ __ SET ON WHAT
26 22 27 14 35

THAT NATURE __ __ __ __ __ __ __;
14 15 35 22 34 15 35

BUT THOSE WHO LIVE IN

ACCORDANCE WITH THE __ __ __ __ __ __
35 32 22 34 22 36

HAVE THEIR MINDS SET ON WHAT THE

SPIRIT __ __ __ __ __ __ __."
14 15 35 22 34 15 35

ROMANS 8:5

91

COLOR *the* PICTURE

"FOR TO BE CARNALLY MINDED IS DEATH; BUT TO BE SPIRITUALLY MINDED IS LIFE AND PEACE. BECAUSE THE CARNAL MIND IS ENMITY AGAINST GOD: FOR IT IS NOT SUBJECT TO THE LAW OF GOD, NEITHER INDEED CAN BE."

ROMANS 8:6-7, KJV

SCRAMBLED VERSES

UNSCRAMBLE THE WORDS BELOW AND COMPLETE THE VERSE ON THE NEXT PAGE.

"UYO, RHEOVWE, ERA DCEOLNLTOR

TON YB ETH LSUINF ENRAUT UBT YB

EHT TSIPRI, FI ETH TSIPRI FO DGO

SLEIV NI UYO."

"— — —,   — — — — — — —,

— — —   — — — — — — — — —

— — —   — —   — — —

— — — — —   — — — — —

— — —   — —   — — —

— — — — — —,   — —   — — —

— — — — — —   — —   — — —

— — — — —   — —   — — —."

ROMANS 8:9

DOUBLE *the* FUN

UNSCRAMBLE THE UNDERLINED WORDS IN EACH VERSE. ON THE NEXT PAGE, PLACE YOUR ANSWERS IN THE SPACES PROVIDED AND THEN COMPLETE THE CROSSWORD PUZZLE.

1. "BUT IF TCSHIR IS IN YOU, YOUR BODY IS DADE BECAUSE OF SIN, YET YOUR RSPITI IS EAVLI BECAUSE OF RIGHTEOUSNESS."

ROMANS 8:10

2. "AND IF THE SPIRIT OF HIM WHO DRAESI JESUS FROM THE DEAD IS LIVING IN YOU, HE WHO RAISED CHRIST FROM THE DEAD WILL ALSO GIVE IFEL TO YOUR LMAOTR SDIEOB THROUGH HIS SPIRIT, WHO LIVES IN YOU."

ROMANS 8:11

1. _____ _____

   _____ _____

2. _____ _____

   _____ _____

FINISH *the* VERSE

USE THE CODE CHART BELOW TO FINISH THE
VERSE ON THE NEXT PAGE. (EXAMPLE: K=24)

	1	2	3	4	5	6	7
1	A	B	C	D	E	F	G
2	H	I	J	K	L	M	N
3	O	P	Q	R	S	T	U
4	V	W	X	Y	Z		

"FOR YOU DID NOT

___ ___ ___ ___ ___ ___ ___ A
34 15 13 15 22 41 15

___ ___ ___ ___ ___ ___ THAT MAKES
35 32 22 34 22 36

YOU A ___ ___ ___ ___ ___ AGAIN TO
      35 25 11 41 15

___ ___ ___ ___, BUT YOU RECEIVED
16 15 11 34

THE ___ ___ ___ ___ ___ ___ OF
    35 32 22 34 22 36

___ ___ ___ ___ ___ ___ ___. AND BY
35 31 27 35 21 22 32

HIM WE ___ ___ ___, '___ ___ ___ ___,'
       13 34 44   11 12 12 11

FATHER.'"

ROMANS 8:15

99

CROSSWORD

ROMANS 8:18–20

ACROSS

1. "I CONSIDER THAT OUR PRESENT
   _____."
2. "ARE NOT _____ COMPARING."
3. "_____ THE GLORY."
4. "THAT WILL BE REVEALED IN _____."

DOWN

1. "THE _____ WAITS IN EAGER
   EXPECTATION."
2. "FOR THE _____ OF GOD TO BE REVEALED."
3. "FOR THE CREATION WAS SUBJECTED TO
   _____."
4. "NOT BY ITS OWN _____, BUT BY THE
   WILL OF THE ONE WHO SUBJECTED IT."

101

SCRAMBLED VERSES

UNSCRAMBLE THE WORDS BELOW AND COMPLETE THE VERSE ON THE NEXT PAGE.

"EW NKWO ATHT ETH EWLHO

CNROAITE SHA NBEE RGNAONIG SA

NI EHT NSPIA FO DCHLIHBTRI TRHIG

PU OT EHT TPNRESE EITM."

"___ __   ___ ___ ___   ___ ___ ___

___ ___ ___   ___ ___ ___ ___

___ ___ ___ ___ ___ ___ ___   ___ ___

___ ___ ___   ___ ___ ___ ___ ___ ___

___ __   ___ __   ___ ___   ___ ___ ___

___ __   ___ ___ ___ ___ ___ ___ ___ ___

___ ___ ___ ___   ___ ___   ___ ___   ___ ___

___ ___ ___ ___ ___ ___   ___ ___ ___ ___."

ROMANS 8:22

103

SECRET CODES

TO SOLVE THE CODED VERSE BELOW, LOOK
AT EACH LETTER AND WRITE THE ONE THAT
COMES BEFORE IT IN THE ALPHABET.

"OPU POMZ TP, CVU XF PVSTFMWFT,

XIP IBWF UIF GJSTUGSVJUT PG UIF

TQJSJU, HSPBO JOXBSEMZ BT XF

XBJU FBHFSMZ GPS PVS BEPQUJPO

BT TPOT, UIF SFEFNQUJPO PG PVS

CPEJFT."

A B C D E F G H I J K L M N O P Q R S T
U V W X Y Z

"__ __ __   __ __ __ __   __ __,
__ __ __   __ __   __ __ __-
__ __ __ __ __ __,   __ __ __
__ __ __ __   __ __ __   __ __ __ __ __ __-
__ __ __ __ __ __ __ __   __ __ __   __ __
__ __ __ __ __ __,   __ __ __ __ __
__ __ __ __ __ __   __ __   __ __
__ __ __ __   __ __ __ __ __ __
__ __ __ __   __ __ __ __   __ __ __ __ __-
__ __ __ __ __   __ __   __ __ __ __ __,
__ __ __   __ __ __ __ __ __ __-
__ __ __ __ __   __ __   __ __ __ __
__ __ __ __ __ __."

ROMANS 8:23

105

FILL *in the* BLANKS

USING THE WORDS BELOW, COMPLETE THE VERSES ON THE NEXT PAGE.

MAN
PATIENCE
NOT
WHY

SEEN
SAVED
WHAT
HOPE

"FOR WE ARE _____ BY HOPE: BUT _____ THAT
IS _____ IS NOT HOPE: FOR _____ A ___ SEETH,
___ DOTH HE YET HOPE FOR? BUT IF WE HOPE
FOR THAT WE SEE ___, THEN DO WE WITH
_____ WAIT FOR IT."

ROMANS 8:24–25, KJV

DOUBLE *the* FUN

UNSCRAMBLE THE UNDERLINED WORDS IN EACH VERSE. ON THE NEXT PAGE, PLACE YOUR ANSWERS IN THE SPACES PROVIDED AND THEN COMPLETE THE CROSSWORD PUZZLE.

1. "IN THE SAME WAY, THE SPIRIT HELPS US IN OUR SWESAENK."

ROMANS 8:26

2. "WE DO NOT KNOW WHAT WE OUGHT TO YPAR FOR, BUT THE SPIRIT FHLIEMS INTERCEDES FOR US WITH SGNRAO THAT SWDOR CANNOT EXPRESS."

ROMANS 8:26

3. "AND HE WHO SSEAEHRC OUR HEARTS KNOWS THE MIND OF THE TSIRIP, BECAUSE THE SPIRIT SIENDTEECR FOR THE SAINTS IN ACCORDANCE WITH GOD'S WILL."

ROMANS 8:27

1. _____

2. _____   _____

   _____   _____

3. _____   _____

   _____

WORD SEARCH

FIND THE WORDS UNDERLINED BELOW IN THE WORD SEARCH ON THE NEXT PAGE.

"AND HE THAT SEARCHETH THE HEARTS KNOWETH WHAT IS THE MIND OF THE SPIRIT, BECAUSE HE MAKETH INTERCESSION FOR THE SAINTS ACCORDING TO THE WILL OF GOD."

ROMANS 8:27, KJV

```
H E A R T S S B X S R D
T G S J V T K F L T R T
G S D B N O T E S S I S
D P E I O I B V D H N E
O T A L R U M I L I T A
R S Z I F B B D M E E R
F W P C T I N E G B R C
K S A P P B S N Z C C H
L Q L R V B I H K T E E
K M W I B D C T I N S T
V N T Y R C E W E S S H
T C O O C E I T T U I W
O T C E R H K B R Z O B
K C C P D V D T R E N L
A R Q O Y C L W I L L R
```

SCRAMBLED VERSES

UNSCRAMBLE THE WORDS BELOW AND COMPLETE THE VERSE ON THE NEXT PAGE.

"DNA EW WNKO THTA NI LAL STGHNI DGO SKRWO RFO EHT DGOO FO ETHSO OWH ELVO MHI, OHW EVHA NEBE DCAELL GANCICDOR OT SHI EPSUORP."

"_ _ _ _ _ _ _ _ _
_ _ _ _ _ _ _ _ _
_ _ _ _ _ _ _ _
_ _ _ _ _ _ _ _ _
_ _ _ _ _ _ _ _ _
_ _ _ _ _ _ _ _ _,
_ _ _ _ _ _ _ _ _
_ _ _ _ _ _ _ _ -
_ _ _ _ _ _ _ _ _
_ _ _ _ _ _."

ROMANS 8:28

FILL *in the* BLANKS

USING THE WORDS BELOW, COMPLETE THE
VERSE ON THE NEXT PAGE.

FIRSTBORN	FOREKNOW
MIGHT	PREDESTINATE
IMAGE	SON
CONFORMED	BRETHREN

"FOR WHOM HE DID _____, HE ALSO DID
_____ TO BE _____ TO THE _____
OF HIS ___, THAT HE _____ BE THE _____
AMONG MANY _____."

ROMANS 8:29, KJV

DOUBLE *the* FUN

UNSCRAMBLE THE UNDERLINED WORDS IN
EACH VERSE. ON THE NEXT PAGE, PLACE YOUR
ANSWERS IN THE SPACES PROVIDED AND
THEN COMPLETE THE CROSSWORD PUZZLE.

1. "AND THOSE HE <u>DPREDENESIT</u>, HE
ALSO CALLED; THOSE HE CALLED, HE ALSO
<u>DJEUSITFI</u>; THOSE HE JUSTIFIED, HE
ALSO <u>GDELOIRIF</u>."

ROMANS 8:30

2. "WHAT, THEN, <u>LALSH</u> WE SAY IN
RESPONSE TO <u>ISHT</u>?"

ROMANS 8:31

3. "IF <u>DGO</u> IS FOR US, WHO CAN BE
<u>ATGSANI</u> US?"

ROMANS 8:31

116

1. _____ _____

_____

2. _____ _____

3. _____ _____

FINISH *the* VERSE

USE THE CODE CHART BELOW TO FINISH THE
VERSE ON THE NEXT PAGE. (EXAMPLE: K=24)

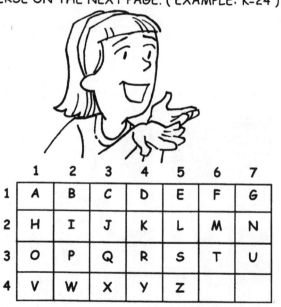

	1	2	3	4	5	6	7
1	A	B	C	D	E	F	G
2	H	I	J	K	L	M	N
3	O	P	Q	R	S	T	U
4	V	W	X	Y	Z		

"HE WHO DID __ __ __
27 31 36

__ __ __ __ __ HIS OWN
35 32 11 34 15

__ __ __, BUT GAVE __ __ __
35 31 27   21 22 26

UP FOR US __ __ __ —HOW
11 25 25

WILL HE NOT __ __ __ __,
11 25 35 31

ALONG WITH __ __ __,
21 22 26

__ __ __ __ __ __ __ __ __ __
17 34 11 13 22 31 37 35 25 44

GIVE US ALL __ __ __ __ __ __?"
36 21 22 27 17 35

ROMANS 8:32

119

FILL *in the* BLANKS

USING THE WORDS BELOW, COMPLETE THE VERSES ON THE NEXT PAGE.

LORD
CREATURE
PRESENT
DEATH
JESUS
COME

PERSUADED
SEPARATE
ANGELS
POWERS
DEPTH
LOVE

"FOR I AM _____, THAT NEITHER _____,
NOR LIFE, NOR _____, NOR PRINCIPALI-
TIES, NOR _____, NOR THINGS _____, NOR
THINGS TO ____, NOR HEIGHT, NOR _____,
NOR ANY OTHER _____, SHALL BE ABLE TO
_____ US FROM THE ____ OF GOD, WHICH
IS IN CHRIST _____ OUR ____."

ROMANS 8:38–39, KJV

SECRET CODES

TO SOLVE THE CODED VERSE BELOW, LOOK
AT EACH LETTER AND WRITE THE ONE THAT
COMES BEFORE IT IN THE ALPHABET.

"XIBU UIFO TIBMM XF TBZ? UIBU UIF

HFOUJMFT, XIP EJE OPU QVSTVF

SJHIUFPVTOFTT, IBWF PCUBJOFE JU,

B SJHIUFPVTOFTT UIBU JT CZ

GBJUI."

A B C D E F G H I J K L M N O P Q R S T
U V W X Y Z

"＿ ＿＿＿ ＿＿＿＿ ＿＿＿＿＿ ＿

＿＿ ＿＿＿? ＿＿＿＿ ＿＿＿ ＿

＿＿＿＿＿＿＿＿, ＿ ＿ ＿

＿＿＿ ＿＿＿ ＿＿＿＿＿

＿＿＿＿＿＿＿＿＿＿＿＿＿,

＿＿＿＿ ＿＿＿＿＿＿＿

＿＿, ＿ ＿＿＿＿＿＿＿＿ ＿-

＿＿＿＿ ＿＿＿＿ ＿＿ ＿＿

＿＿＿＿＿."

ROMANS 9:30

CROSSWORD

ROMANS 9:31–33

ACROSS

1. "BUT ISRAEL, WHO PURSUED A LAW OF RIGHTEOUSNESS, HAS NOT _____ IT."
2. "WHY NOT? BECAUSE THEY _____ IT NOT BY FAITH."
3. "BUT AS IF IT WERE BY _____."
4. "THEY _____ OVER THE 'STUMBLING STONE.'"

DOWN

1. "AS IT IS WRITTEN: 'SEE, I LAY IN ZION A _____.'"
2. "'THAT CAUSES _____ TO STUMBLE.'"
3. "'AND A ROCK THAT MAKES THEM _____.'"
4. "'AND THE ONE WHO _____ IN HIM WILL NEVER BE PUT TO SHAME.'"

125

SCRAMBLED VERSES

UNSCRAMBLE THE WORDS BELOW AND COMPLETE THE VERSE ON THE NEXT PAGE.

"SBRORETH, YM SHTRAE EDERIS

DAN RPARYE OT DGO RFO ETH

ISSERATIEL SI TAHT YTHE YAM EB

DSVAE."

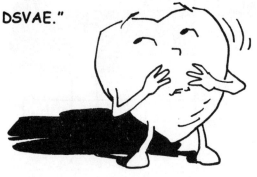

" ____ ____ ____ ____ ____ ____ ____, ____ ____

____ ____ ____ ____ ____ '____ ____ ____ ____ ____

____ ____ ____ ____ ____ ____ ____ ____ ____

____ ____ ____ ____ ____ ____ ____ ____

____ ____ ____ ____ ____ ____ ____ ____ ____

____ ____ ____ ____ ____ ____ ____ ____

____ ____ ____ ____ ____ ____ ____ ____ ."

ROMANS 10:1

FINISH *the* VERSE

USE THE CODE CHART BELOW TO FINISH THE
VERSE ON THE NEXT PAGE. (EXAMPLE: K=24)

	1	2	3	4	5	6	7
1	A	B	C	D	E	F	G
2	H	I	J	K	L	M	N
3	O	P	Q	R	S	T	U
4	V	W	X	Y	Z		

"FOR I CAN _ _ _ _ _ _ _
         36 15 35 36 22 16 44

ABOUT _ _ _ _ THAT THEY
      36 21 15 26

ARE _ _ _ _ _ _ _ FOR
    45 15 11 25 31 37 35

_ _ _, BUT THEIR _ _ _ _
17 31 14   45 15 11 25

IS NOT BASED ON _ _ _ _-
                24 27 31 42

_ _ _ _ _."
25 15 14 17 15

ROMANS 10:2

129

WORD SEARCH

FIND THE WORDS LISTED BELOW IN
THE WORD SEARCH ON THE NEXT PAGE.

COMES

GODS

SOUGHT

ESTABLISH

KNOW

GOD

RIGHTEOUSNES

SUBMIT

```
E  S  T  C  E  P  A  Q  N  S  N  R
G  O  N  M  J  E  B  V  S  M  Q  I
E  U  K  R  P  S  U  B  M  I  T  G
H  G  R  Q  L  Y  V  D  M  F  G  H
K  H  J  G  O  N  C  L  G  P  F  T
Y  T  S  J  G  O  D  S  X  B  F  E
R  A  D  B  E  B  D  F  H  X  A  O
F  P  N  T  P  E  L  S  S  C  T  U
M  G  O  D  R  B  I  C  X  U  F  S
L  R  Z  T  E  L  V  D  H  V  S  N
J  W  A  C  B  R  B  D  M  D  S  E
F  H  A  A  P  I  K  N  O  W  E  S
Z  Q  T  R  V  B  J  D  Z  B  N  S
X  S  W  I  B  B  P  E  K  C  I  D
E  B  Y  D  N  B  C  O  M  E  S  Q
```

COLOR *the* PICTURE

"BEHOLD, I AM LAYING IN ZION A STONE OF STUMBLING, AND A ROCK OF OFFENSE; AND WHOEVER BELIEVES IN HIM WILL NOT BE PUT TO SHAME."

ROMANS 9:33, ESV

133

DOUBLE *the* FUN

UNSCRAMBLE THE UNDERLINED WORDS IN EACH VERSE. ON THE NEXT PAGE, PLACE YOUR ANSWERS IN THE SPACES PROVIDED AND THEN COMPLETE THE CROSSWORD PUZZLE.

1. "FOR CHRIST IS THE END OF THE LAW FOR <u>SEIGORTEHSNSU</u> TO <u>EVNEREYO</u> THAT <u>THEVLEBIE</u>."

ROMANS 10:4, KJV

2. "BUT WHAT SAITH IT? THE <u>DROW</u> IS NIGH THEE, EVEN IN THY MOUTH, AND IN THY <u>THREA</u>: THAT IS, THE WORD OF FAITH, WHICH WE PREACH."

ROMANS 10:8, KJV

3. "THAT IF THOU SHALT <u>SNOCEFS</u> WITH THY <u>OMUHT</u> THE LORD JESUS, AND SHALT BELIEVE IN THINE HEART THAT GOD HATH <u>DREASI</u> HIM FROM THE DEAD, THOU SHALT BE SAVED."

ROMANS 10:9, KJV

1. _____ _____
   _____

2. _____ _____

3. _____ _____
   _____

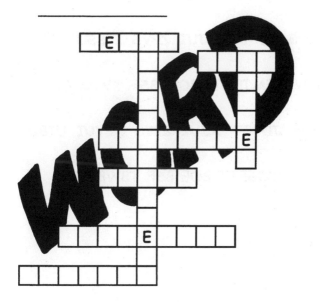

SECRET CODES

TO SOLVE THE CODED VERSE BELOW, LOOK AT EACH LETTER AND WRITE THE ONE THAT COMES BEFORE IT IN THE ALPHABET.

"GPS JU JT XJUI ZPVS IFBSU UIBU

ZPV CFMJFWF BOE BSF KVTUJGJFE,

BOE JU JT XJUI ZPVS NPVUI UIBU

ZPV DPOGFTT BOE BSF TBWFE."

A B C D E F G H I J K L M N O P Q R S T
U V W X Y Z

"__ __ __ __ __ __ __ __ __ __ __

__ __ __ __ __ __ __ __ __ __

__ __ __ __ __ __ __ __ __ __ __

__ __ __ __ __ __ __ __ __ __ __'

__ __ __ __ __ __ __ __ __ __

__ __ __ __ __ __ __ __ __

__ __ __ __ __ __ __ __ __

__ __ __ __ __ __ __ __ __ __."

ROMANS 10:10

FILL *in the* BLANKS

USING THE WORDS BELOW, COMPLETE THE
VERSES ON THE NEXT PAGE.

EVERYONE   CALL
NAME   SHAME
RICHES   ALL
SAME   SAVED
DISTINCTION   BELIEVES
SCRIPTURE   JEW

FOR THE _____ SAYS, "EVERYONE WHO _____ IN HIM WILL NOT BE PUT TO _____." FOR THERE IS NO _____ BETWEEN ___ AND GREEK; FOR THE ____ LORD IS LORD OF ___, BESTOWING HIS _____ ON ALL WHO ____ ON HIM. FOR "_____ WHO CALLS ON THE ____ OF THE LORD WILL BE _____."

ROMANS 10:11–13, ESV

SCRAMBLED VERSES

UNSCRAMBLE THE WORDS BELOW AND COMPLETE THE VERSE ON THE NEXT PAGE.

"I KAS HTNE: IDD DGO JERTEC SHI EPEPOL? YB ON SNMAE! I MA NA SIARLETIE YMESFL, A EDCSNEADTN FO BAARAHM, MFOR EHT RTBIE FO EBJNMANI."

140

"_ _ _ _ _ _ _ _:

_ _ _ _ _ _ _ _ _ _ _

_ _ _ _ _ _ _ _ _?

_ _ _ _ _ _ _ _ _!

_ _ _ _ _ _ _ _ _ _-

_ _ _ _ _ _ _ _ _,

_ _ _ _ _ _ _ _ _ _ _

_ _ _ _ _ _ _ _ _,

_ _ _ _ _ _ _ _ _ _ _

_ _ _ _ _ _ _ _ _."

ROMANS 11:1

FINISH *the* VERSE

USE THE CODE CHART BELOW TO FINISH THE
VERSE ON THE NEXT PAGE. (EXAMPLE: K=24)

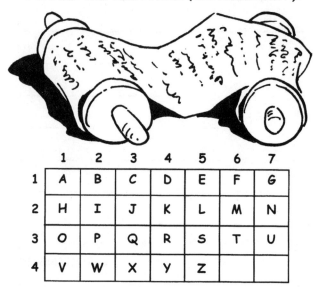

	1	2	3	4	5	6	7
1	A	B	C	D	E	F	G
2	H	I	J	K	L	M	N
3	O	P	Q	R	S	T	U
4	V	W	X	Y	Z		

"_ _ _ DID NOT _ _ _ _ _ _
 17 31 14   34 15 23 15 13 36

HIS _ _ _ _ _ _, WHOM HE
     32 15 31 32 25 15

_ _ _ _ _ _ _ _. DON'T YOU KNOW
16 31 34 15 24 27 15 42

WHAT THE _ _ _ _ _ _ _ _ _
         35 13 34 22 32 36 37 34 15

SAYS IN THE _ _ _ _ _ _ _
               32 11 35 35 11 17 15

ABOUT _ _ _ _ _ _ — HOW HE
      15 25 22 23 11 21

_ _ _ _ _ _ _ _ TO _ _ _
11 32 32 15 11 25 15 14   17 31 14

AGAINST ISRAEL."

ROMANS 11:2

143

CROSSWORD

ROMANS 11:3–5

ACROSS

1. "'LORD, THEY HAVE KILLED YOUR
_____.'"
2. "'AND TORN DOWN YOUR _____.'"
3. "'I AM THE ONLY ONE _____.'"
4. "'AND THEY ARE TRYING TO KILL _____.'"

DOWN

1. "AND WHAT WAS GOD'S _____ TO
HIM?"
2. "'I HAVE _____ FOR MYSELF.'"
3. "'SEVEN THOUSAND WHO HAVE NOT BOWED
THE _____ TO BAAL.'"
4. "SO TOO, AT THE PRESENT _____ THERE IS
A REMNANT CHOSEN BY GRACE."

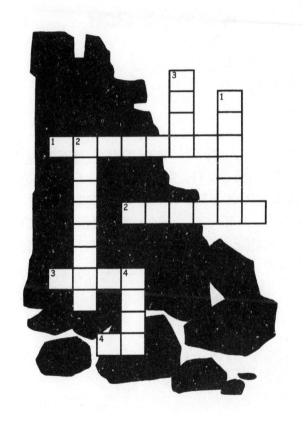

145

WORD SEARCH

FIND THE WORDS UNDERLINED BELOW IN THE WORD SEARCH ON THE NEXT PAGE.

"EVEN SO THEN AT THIS <u>PRESENT</u> <u>TIME</u> ALSO THERE IS A <u>REMNANT</u> ACCORDING TO THE <u>ELECTION</u> OF GRACE. AND IF BY GRACE, THEN IS IT NO <u>MORE</u> OF <u>WORKS</u>: <u>OTHERWISE</u> GRACE IS NO MORE <u>GRACE</u>."

ROMANS 11:5-6, KJV

```
K M W I B B C T I N B O
F B Y D B A Q N N Q S L
T C H E L E C T I O N W
O T H E R S T D E K O B
K M O R E E R T T E U L
H R Q O Y C L N E W L R
F J G O N T E Z S R D D
G S J V B S F L T R T A
S D B E E L E S S E S G
P E T R R S V D H M T R
T P P H K M I L I N Y A
R Z T R B B D M S A N C
W A O T I M E S B N I E
H W P P B S D Z C T L O
Q W O T H E R W I S E N
```

SCRAMBLED VERSES

UNSCRAMBLE THE WORDS BELOW AND COMPLETE THE VERSE ON THE NEXT PAGE.

"HTREFEORE, I RUEG UOY, RBTOEHSR,

NI IVEW FO DGOS YMREC, OT FOFRE

OURY   OBDEIS   SA   ILIVGN

ASRCFICISE, OHYL NAD LPAESNIG OT

DGO—HTSI SI RYUO ISPIRUTLA CAT

FO OWRHSPI."

"_ _ _ _ _ _ _ _ _ _,
_ _ _ _ _ _ _ _,
_ _ _ _ _ _ _ _, _ _
_ _ _ _ _ _ _ _ _
_ _ _ _ _, _ _ _ _ _ _
_ _ _ _ _ _ _ _ _
_ _ _ _ _ _ _ _ _ _ _ -
_ _ _ _ _, _ _ _ _ _ _ _
_ _ _ _ _ _ _ _ _ _ _ _
_ _ _ _ _ _ _ _ _
_ _ _ _ _ _ _ _ _ _ _
_ _ _ _ _ _ _ _ _."

ROMANS 12:1

149

FILL *in the* BLANKS

USING THE WORDS BELOW, COMPLETE THE VERSE ON THE NEXT PAGE.

ACCEPTABLE   RENEWING
GOOD   WORLD
PROVE   CONFORMED
WILL   GOD
MIND   TRANSFORMED

"AND BE NOT _____ TO THIS _____: BUT
BE YE _____ BY THE _____ OF YOUR
_____, THAT YE MAY _____ WHAT IS THAT _____,
AND _____, AND PERFECT, _____ OF ____."

ROMANS 12:2, KJV

CROSSWORD

ROMANS 12:9–11

ACROSS

1. "LOVE MUST BE _____."
2. "HATE WHAT IS _____."
3. "_____ TO WHAT IS GOOD."
4. "BE DEVOTED TO _____ ANOTHER."

DOWN

1. "IN _____ LOVE."
2. "HONOR ONE _____ ABOVE YOURSELVES."
3. "_____ BE LACKING IN ZEAL."
4. "BUT KEEP YOUR _____ FERVOR, SERVING THE LORD."

153

SECRET CODES

TO SOLVE THE CODED VERSES BELOW, LOOK
AT EACH LETTER AND WRITE THE ONE THAT
COMES BEFORE IT IN THE ALPHABET.

"CMFTT UIPTF XIP QFSTFDVUF ZPV;

CMFTT BOE EP OPU DVSTF. SFKPJDF

XJUI UIPTF XIP SFKPJDF; NPVSO

XJUI UIPTF XIP NPVSO."

A B C D E F G H I J K L M N O P Q R S T
U V W X Y Z

"_ _ _ _ _ _ _ _ _ _ _ _ _

_ _ _ _ _ _ _ _   _ _ _;

_ _ _ _ _ _ _ _ _ _ _ _ _

_ _ _ _ _. _ _ _ _ _ _ _

_ _ _ _ _ _ _ _ _ _ _ _

_ _ _ _ _ _ _; _ _ _ _

_ _ _ _ _ _ _ _ _ _ _ _

_ _ _ _ _."

ROMANS 12:14–15

155

FINISH *the* VERSE

USE THE CODE CHART BELOW TO FINISH THE VERSE ON THE NEXT PAGE. (EXAMPLE: K=24)

	1	2	3	4	5	6	7
1	A	B	C	D	E	F	G
2	H	I	J	K	L	M	N
3	O	P	Q	R	S	T	U
4	V	W	X	Y	Z		

"ON THE __ __ __ __ __ __ __ __:
     13 31 27 36 34 11 34 44

IF   YOUR   __ __ __ __ __   IS
             15 27 15 26 44

__ __ __ __ __ __,   __ __ __ __
21 37 27 17 34 44   16 15 15 14

HIM; IF HE IS __ __ __ __ __ __ __,
              36 21 22 34 35 36 44

GIVE __ __ __   SOMETHING   TO
     21 22 26

__ __ __ __ __. IN __ __ __ __ __
14 34 22 27 24   14 31 22 27 17

THIS, YOU __ __ __ __   __ __ __ __
          42 22 25 25   21 15 11 32

__ __ __ __ __ __ __   __ __ __ __ __
12 37 34 27 22 27 17   13 31 11 25 35

ON HIS __ __ __ __."
       21 15 11 14

ROMANS 12:20

DOUBLE *the* FUN

UNSCRAMBLE THE UNDERLINED WORDS IN EACH VERSE. ON THE NEXT PAGE, PLACE YOUR ANSWERS IN THE SPACES PROVIDED AND THEN COMPLETE THE CROSSWORD PUZZLE.

"VENOREYE MUST TSIUMB FLIMESH TO THE OGINGREVN AUTHORITIES, FOR THERE IS NO AUTHORITY TEPCXE THAT WHICH GOD HAS EDEHSILBATS. THE SEITIROHTUA THAT EXIST HAVE NEBE ESTABLISHED BY ODG."

ROMANS 13:1

159

COLOR *the* PICTURE

"BUT PUT YE ON THE LORD JESUS CHRIST, AND MAKE NOT PROVISION FOR THE FLESH, TO FULFIL THE LUSTS THEREOF."

ROMANS 13:14, KJV

FINISH *the* VERSE

USE THE CODE CHART BELOW TO FINISH THE
VERSE ON THE NEXT PAGE. (EXAMPLE: K=24)

	1	2	3	4	5	6	7
1	A	B	C	D	E	F	G
2	H	I	J	K	L	M	N
3	O	P	Q	R	S	T	U
4	V	W	X	Y	Z		

"ACCEPT __ __ __ WHOSE
          21 22 26

__ __ __ __ __ IS __ __ __ __,
16 11 22 36 21   42 15 11 24

WITHOUT __ __ __ __ __ __ __
         32 11 35 35 22 27 17

__ __ __ __ __ __ __ __
23 37 14 17 26 15 27 36

ON __ __ __ __ __ __ __ __ __ __
   14 22 35 32 37 36 11 12 25 15

MATTERS."

ROMANS 14:1

163

FILL *in the* BLANKS

USING THE WORDS BELOW, COMPLETE THE
VERSE ON THE NEXT PAGE.

THINGS
LORD
RIGHT
HELP
PLEASE

BUILD
SENSITIVE
STRONG
CONSIDERATE
MUST

164

"WE WHO ARE _____ MUST BE _____ OF THOSE WHO ARE _____ ABOUT _____ LIKE THIS. WE ____ NOT JUST _____ OUR-SELVES. WE SHOULD ____ OTHERS DO WHAT IS _____ AND _____ THEM UP IN THE ____."

ROMANS 15:1-2, NLT

SECRET CODES

TO SOLVE THE CODED VERSE BELOW, LOOK
AT EACH LETTER AND WRITE THE ONE THAT
COMES BEFORE IT IN THE ALPHABET.

"GPS FWFO DISJTU EJE OPU QMFBTF

IJNTFMG CVU, BT JU JT XSJUUFO:

'UIF JOTVMUT PG UIPTF XIP JOTVMU

ZPV IBWF GBMMFO PO NF.'"

A B C D E F G H I J K L M N O P Q R S T
U V W X Y Z

"___ ____ _____

___ ___ _____

_____ _ ___ ___,'

__ __ __ _____;

'___ _____ __

____ ___ _____

___ ____ _____

__ __ _.'"

ROMANS 15:3

FILL *in the* BLANKS

USING THE WORDS BELOW, COMPLETE THE
VERSE ON THE NEXT PAGE.

POWER   GOD
GHOST   JOY
HOPE   ABOUND
BELIEVING   YE
FILL   THROUGH

"NOW THE ___ OF HOPE ____ YOU WITH ALL ___ AND PEACE IN _____, THAT __ MAY _____ IN ____, _____ THE _____ OF THE HOLY _____."

ROMANS 15:13, KJV

COLOR *the* PICTURE

"WE THEN THAT ARE STRONG OUGHT TO BEAR THE INFIRMITIES OF THE WEAK, AND NOT TO PLEASE OURSELVES. LET EVERY ONE OF US PLEASE HIS NEIGHBOUR FOR HIS GOOD TO EDIFICATION. FOR EVEN CHRIST PLEASED NOT HIMSELF; BUT, AS IT IS WRITTEN, THE REPROACHES OF THEM THAT REPROACHED THEE FELL ON ME."

ROMANS 15:1–3, KJV

COLOR THE PICTURE

WHAT IS GRACE?

GOD'S WORD MAKES USE OF VERY HELPFUL TOOLS FOR TEACHING: *CONTRASTS*. THERE ARE CONTRASTS BETWEEN LIGHT AND DARKNESS, THE KINGDOM OF GOD AND THE KINGDOM OF SATAN, LIFE AND DEATH, LOST AND SAVED, AND *LAW AND GRACE*.

LAW AND GRACE ARE THE VERY HEART OF THE GOSPEL—THE DIFFERENCE BETWEEN THE TWO WILL DECIDE IF A PERSON IS SAVED AND HOW HE WILL LIVE THE CHRISTIAN LIFE.

IN ORDER TO UNDERSTAND WHAT GRACE REALLY IS, WE NEED TO KNOW WHAT THE LAW IS.

IN THIS BOOK, WE WILL LOOK AT BOTH OF THEM SO THAT WE MIGHT COMPLETELY UNDERSTAND *THE GRACE OF GOD*.

CROSS 'EM OUT

ON THE NEXT PAGE, CROSS OUT ALL THE
LETTERS THAT APPEAR IN THE BOX FOUR
TIMES. COMPLETE THE VERSE BY PLACING
THE LETTERS THAT ARE LEFT OVER, AS THEY
APPEAR, IN THE SPACES PROVIDED.

```
H  O  F  R  L  C  I  M  T
D  B  T  J  G  N  Q  A  K
I  P  M  V  O  H  D  P  F
C  R  A  K  T  E  R  V  B
L  S  W  H  W  V  W  G  Q
Q  P  N  W  L  B  O  C  I
F  G  V  D  T  R  A  N  U
K  A  I  Q  M  O  H  P  L
M  C  N  S  G  B  K  D  F
```

"FOR THE LAW WAS GIVEN BY MOSES, BUT
GRACE AND TRUTH CAME BY ___ ___ ___ ___ ___
CHRIST."

JOHN 1:17, KJV

FILL in the BLANKS

USING THE WORDS BELOW, COMPLETE THE VERSES ON THE NEXT PAGE.

GRACE   SAVED
BELIEVE   GOD
WAY   BEAR
ANCESTORS   YOKE
GENTILE   LORD
NOW   NEITHER

"SO WHY ARE YOU _____ CHALLENGING _____ BY BURDENING THE GENTILE BELIEVERS WITH A _____ THAT _____ WE NOR OUR _____ WERE ABLE TO _____? WE _____ THAT WE ARE ALL _____ THE SAME _____, BY THE UNDESERVED _____ OF THE _____ JESUS."

ACTS 15:10–11, NLT

SCRAMBLED CIRCLES

ON THE NEXT PAGE, UNSCRAMBLE THE WORDS IN THE LIST BELOW. THEN USE THE CIRCLED LETTERS TO COMPLETE THE VERSE.

1. EMCA
2. SMEOS
3. VINGE
4. YTR
5. RTCSIH
6. KECSN
7. OYU
8. UJSES

1. ◯ _ _ _
2. _ ◯ _ _ _
3. _ _ _ _ ◯
4. ◯ _ _
5. _ _ _ ◯ _ _
6. ◯ _ _ _ _
7. _ _ ◯
8. _ ◯ _ _ _

"SO THEN, JUST AS YOU RECEIVED CHRIST JESUS AS LORD, _ _ _ _ _ _ _ _ TO LIVE IN HIM."

COLOSSIANS 2:6

179

DOUBLE the FUN

UNSCRAMBLE THE UNDERLINED WORDS IN EACH VERSE. ON THE NEXT PAGE, PLACE YOUR ANSWERS IN THE SPACES PROVIDED AND THEN COMPLETE THE CROSSWORD PUZZLE.

1. "NOW IF THE SNIYTIRM THAT BROUGHT DEATH, WHICH WAS REDNAVEG IN LETTERS ON STONE, CAME WITH OLRGY, SO THAT THE ISRAELITES COULD NOT LOOK DETLIASY AT THE FACE OF MOSES BECAUSE OF ITS GLORY, FADING THOUGH IT WAS, WILL NOT THE MINISTRY OF THE SPIRIT BE EVEN MORE GLORIOUS?"

   2 CORINTHIANS 3:7–8

2. "IF THE MINISTRY THAT NENSDCMO MEN IS GLORIOUS, HOW MUCH REMO GLORIOUS IS THE MINISTRY THAT BRINGS RIGHTEOUSNESS!"

   2 CORINTHIANS 3:9

3. "RFO WHAT WAS GLORIOUS HAS NO GLORY NOW IN ROIONMCPSA WITH THE SURPASSING GLORY."

   2 CORINTHIANS 3:10

1. _____   _____

   _____   _____

2. _____   _____

3. _____   _____

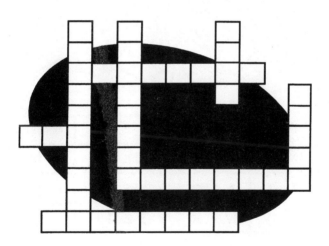

FINISH the VERSE

USE THE CODE CHART BELOW TO FINISH THE
VERSES ON THE NEXT PAGE. (EXAMPLE: K=24)

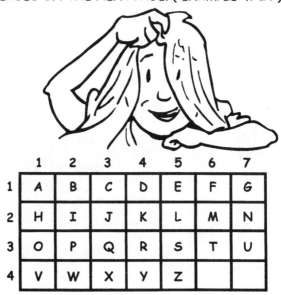

	1	2	3	4	5	6	7
1	A	B	C	D	E	F	G
2	H	I	J	K	L	M	N
3	O	P	Q	R	S	T	U
4	V	W	X	Y	Z		

"NOW THE __ __ __ __ IS THE
     25 31 34 14

__ __ __ __ __ __, AND WHERE THE
35 32 22 34 22 36

SPIRIT OF THE LORD IS, THERE IS

__ __ __ __ __ __ __. AND WE, WHO
16 34 15 15 14 31 26

WITH UNVEILED __ __ __ __ __ ALL
        16 11 13 15 35

__ __ __ __ __ __ __ THE LORD'S
34 15 16 25 15 13 36

__ __ __ __ __, ARE BEING
17 25 31 34 44

TRANSFORMED INTO HIS

__ __ __ __ __ __ __ __ WITH EVER-
25 22 24 15 27 15 35 35

INCREASING GLORY, WHICH

__ __ __ __ __ FROM THE
13 31 26 15 35

__ __ __ __, WHO IS THE SPIRIT."
25 31 34 14

2 CORINTHIANS 3:17–18

183

CROSS 'EM OUT

ON THE NEXT PAGE, CROSS OUT ALL THE LETTERS THAT APPEAR IN THE BOX FOUR TIMES. COMPLETE THE VERSE BY PLACING THE LETTERS THAT ARE LEFT OVER, AS THEY APPEAR, IN THE SPACES PROVIDED.

```
D J E M B Q L P E
N C U I O K G W S
K S P V X D S N V
O R F L M V F C J
F G Q X D U I B P
J L A K V O Q M C
N U M C S X L T G
B E O I U K Q I N
P G X D H F E J B
```

"FOR WHICH THINGS' SAKE THE __ __ __ __ __

OF GOD COMETH ON THE CHILDREN OF

DISOBEDIENCE."

COLOSSIANS 3:6, KJV

ASK YOURSELF

WHAT HAVE YOU LEARNED SO FAR? FIND OUT
BY ANSWERING THE QUESTIONS BELOW.

1. WHAT WAS GIVEN THROUGH
MOSES?

JOHN 1:17

_____

2. WHAT CAME THROUGH JESUS
CHRIST?

JOHN 1:17

_____

3. GOD MADE PAUL A COMPETENT
MINISTER OF WHAT?

2 CORINTHIANS 3:6

_____

4. IS THE COVENANT OF THE LETTER OR OF THE SPIRIT?

2 CORINTHIANS 3:6

_____

5. WHAT DOES THE LETTER DO?

2 CORINTHIANS 3:6

_____

6. WHAT DOES THE SPIRIT DO?

2 CORINTHIANS 3:6

_____

COLOR THE PICTURE

A CLOSER LOOK AT THE LAW

THE BIBLE WILL SHOW US THAT THE LAW IS MADE UP OF THE *TEN COMMANDMENTS* AND THE CEREMONIAL LAWS GIVEN TO MOSES AT MOUNT SINAI.

THE GRACE OF JESUS CHRIST IS FAR GREATER THAN THE LAW THAT WAS GIVEN AT MOUNT SINAI. SO, WHY WAS THE LAW GIVEN?

THE LAW THAT GOD GAVE WAS FOR THE NATION OF ISRAEL SO THAT THEY WOULD PROSPER AND LIVE. WITH THE SACRIFICES THAT WERE NEEDED, IN THE LAW, THE PEOPLE OF ISRAEL WERE GIVEN A WAY OF HAVING THEIR SINS COVERED FOR A TIME.

BUT GOD HAS SOMETHING BETTER FOR YOU AND ME. THE ONLY PURPOSE FOR THE LAW TODAY IS A *SPIRITUAL* ONE—IT LEADS US TO JESUS CHRIST.

FILL in the BLANKS

USING THE WORDS BELOW, COMPLETE THE
VERSES ON THE NEXT PAGE.

VOICE   WINGS
BORE   COVENANT
MYSELF   OBEY
YOURSELVES   PEOPLES
EGYPTIANS   THEREFORE

"YOU _____ HAVE SEEN WHAT I DID
TO THE _____, AND HOW I ____ YOU ON
EAGLES' _____ AND BROUGHT YOU TO _____.
NOW _____, IF YOU WILL INDEED ____
MY _____ AND KEEP MY _____, YOU SHALL
BE MY TREASURED POSSESSION AMONG ALL
_____, FOR ALL THE EARTH IS MINE."

EXODUS 19:4-5, ESV

CROSSWORD

ROMANS 5:6-8

ACROSS

1. "YOU SEE, AT JUST THE _____ TIME."
2. "WHEN WE WERE STILL _____."
3. "_____ DIED FOR THE UNGODLY."
4. "VERY RARELY WILL ANYONE DIE FOR A _____ MAN."

DOWN

1. "_____ FOR A GOOD MAN SOMEONE MIGHT POSSIBLY DARE TO DIE."
2. "BUT GOD _____ HIS OWN LOVE FOR US IN THIS."
3. "WHILE WE WERE STILL _____."
4. "CHRIST DIED FOR ____."

193

CROSS 'EM OUT

ON THE NEXT PAGE, CROSS OUT ALL THE
LETTERS THAT APPEAR IN THE BOX FOUR
TIMES. COMPLETE THE VERSE BY PLACING
THE LETTERS THAT ARE LEFT OVER, AS THEY
APPEAR, IN THE SPACES PROVIDED.

```
G   M   J   Q   H   O   D   I   P
R   C   F   W   K   Z   U   W   R
K   T   N   Z   P   B   J   Q   M
D   I   U   S   T   R   F   Z   W
O   B   H   C   Z   G   N   C   D
P   G   J   Q   F   W   J   L   O
T   N   F   U   P   H   A   U   T
V   C   O   R   M   N   G   I   B
K   I   E   H   D   B   M   K   Q
```

"SO THE TROUBLE IS NOT WITH THE LAW, FOR
IT IS SPIRITUAL AND GOOD. THE TROUBLE
IS WITH ME, FOR I AM ALL TOO HUMAN,
A ___ ___ ___ ___ ___ TO SIN."

ROMANS 7:14, NLT

195

SCRAMBLED CIRCLES

ON THE NEXT PAGE, UNSCRAMBLE THE WORDS IN THE LIST BELOW. THEN USE THE CIRCLED LETTERS TO COMPLETE THE VERSE.

1. LDSO

2. ERDA

3. IHRTCS

4. WLA

5. VATNOENC

6. LARYRE

7. GEELA

8. EDDI

1. _ _ _◯

2. _ _ _◯

3. ◯_ _ _ _ _

4. ◯_ _

5. _ _ _ _ _◯_ _

6. _ _◯_ _ _

7. ◯_ _ _ _

8. _ _ _◯

"THEREFORE   NO   ONE   WILL   BE
_ _ _ _ _ _ _ _ _   RIGHTEOUS IN
HIS SIGHT BY OBSERVING THE LAW;
RATHER, THROUGH THE LAW WE BECOME
CONSCIOUS OF SIN."

ROMANS 3:20

197

FINISH THE VERSE

USE THE CODE CHART BELOW TO FINISH THE VERSE ON THE NEXT PAGE. (EXAMPLE: K=24)

	1	2	3	4	5	6	7
1	A	B	C	D	E	F	G
2	H	I	J	K	L	M	N
3	O	P	Q	R	S	T	U
4	V	W	X	Y	Z		

"IF YOU $\underline{}_{16}$ $\underline{}_{37}$ $\underline{}_{25}$ $\underline{}_{25}$ $\underline{}_{44}$ OBEY THE

LORD YOUR $\underline{}_{17}$ $\underline{}_{31}$ $\underline{}_{14}$ AND CAREFULLY

$\underline{}_{16}$ $\underline{}_{31}$ $\underline{}_{25}$ $\underline{}_{25}$ $\underline{}_{31}$ $\underline{}_{42}$ ALL HIS

$\underline{}_{13}$ $\underline{}_{31}$ $\underline{}_{26}$ $\underline{}_{26}$ $\underline{}_{11}$ $\underline{}_{27}$ $\underline{}_{14}$ $\underline{}_{35}$ I GIVE YOU

TODAY, THE $\underline{}_{25}$ $\underline{}_{31}$ $\underline{}_{34}$ $\underline{}_{14}$ YOUR GOD

WILL SET YOU $\underline{}_{21}$ $\underline{}_{22}$ $\underline{}_{17}$ $\underline{}_{21}$ ABOVE

ALL THE $\underline{}_{27}$ $\underline{}_{11}$ $\underline{}_{36}$ $\underline{}_{22}$ $\underline{}_{31}$ $\underline{}_{27}$ $\underline{}_{35}$ ON

EARTH."

DEUTERONOMY 28:1

SCRAMBLED VERSES

UNSCRAMBLE THE WORDS BELOW AND
COMPLETE THE VERSE ON THE NEXT PAGE.

"WVEHOER, FI UYO OD TNO EYBO

HET RLDO UROY DGO DAN OD TON

EUAYLRLCF OLFWLO LAL SHI

AOCMNDMS NAD RSEECDE I MA

NIGVGI UOY YTAOD, LAL EEHST

SRESCU ILWL ECMO OUNP OYU ADN

AERTOVEK UYO."

200

"_____, ___ ___

___ ___ ___ ___ ___

___ ___ ___ ___ ___

___ ___ ___ ___ ___

___ ___ ___ ___

___ ___ ___ ___

___ ___ ___ ___

___ ___ ___ ___

___ ___ ___ ___ ___

___ ___ ___ ___

___ ___ ___."

DEUTERONOMY 28:15

SECRET CODES

TO SOLVE THE CODED VERSE BELOW, LOOK
AT EACH LETTER AND WRITE THE ONE THAT
COMES BEFORE IT IN THE ALPHABET.

"XIBU, UIFO, XBT UIF QVSQPTF PG
UIF MBX? JU XBT BEEFE CFDBVTF PG
USBOTHSFTTJPOT VOUJM UIF TFFE
UP XIPN UIF QSPNJTF SFGFSSFE
IBE DPNF. UIF MBX XBT QVU JOUP
FGGFDU UISPVHI BOHFMT CZ B
NFEJBUPS."

A B C D E F G H I J K L M N O P Q R S T
U V W X Y Z

"_____, _____, _____

_____ _____ _____

_____ _____? _____ _____

_____ _____ _____

_____

_____ _____ _____

_____ _____ _____

_____ _____

_____ _____. _____ _____

_____ _____ _____

_____ _____

_____ _____ _____

_____."

GALATIANS 3:19

203

DOUBLE the FUN

UNSCRAMBLE THE UNDERLINED WORDS IN
EACH VERSE. ON THE NEXT PAGE, PLACE YOUR
ANSWERS IN THE SPACES PROVIDED AND
THEN COMPLETE THE CROSSWORD PUZZLE.

1. "SO THEN, THE LAW IS <u>LOYH</u>, AND THE
<u>MDNEACMNTOM</u> IS HOLY, <u>TGSOIRUHE</u>
AND <u>ODGO</u>."

ROMANS 7:12

2. "WE KNOW THAT THE LAW IS <u>IARLSIUTP</u>;
BUT I AM <u>RSUATILPNUI</u>, SOLD AS A
<u>EVLSA</u> TO <u>NSI</u>."

ROMANS 7:14

204

1. _____ _____

   _____ _____

2. _____ _____

   _____ _____

ASK YOURSELF

WHAT HAVE YOU LEARNED SO FAR? FIND OUT BY ANSWERING THE QUESTIONS BELOW.

1. WHAT DID MOSES WRITE DOWN?

   EXODUS 24:4–8

   _____

2. HOW LONG WAS THE LAW TO BE IN EFFECT FOR ISRAEL?

   GALATIANS 3:19

   _____

3. WHAT DO YOU THINK THE SEED REFERS TO?

   GALATIANS 3:19

   _____

4. HOW DOES PAUL DESCRIBE THE LAW?

ROMANS 7:12–14

_____

5. IS THE LAW SPIRITUAL OR PHYSICAL?

ROMANS 7:12–14

_____

6. DOES THE LAW HAVE A SPIRITUAL PURPOSE IN OUR LIVES?

ROMANS 3:20

_____

COLOR THE PICTURE

THE PURPOSE OF THE LAW

THE LAW DOES HAVE A PURPOSE—IT IS A SPIRITUAL PURPOSE.

THE PURPOSE IS FOUND IN THE QUESTION, "WHO TURNS TO JESUS CHRIST FOR SALVATION?" ONLY THOSE WHO KNOW THEY NEED TO BE SAVED.

THE LAW IS LIKE A TEACHER. IT TEACHES US THE DIFFERENCE BETWEEN RIGHT AND WRONG; IT TEACHES US ABOUT ACTIONS AND THOUGHTS AND ATTITUDES THAT ARE SEEN AS SIN IN GOD'S EYES. IT HELPS US TO UNDERSTAND THE PERFECT REQUIREMENTS OF GOD FOR HOLINESS AND RIGHTEOUSNESS.

BUT *THIS PERFECTION* WE CAN NEVER MEET.

CROSS 'EM OUT

ON THE NEXT PAGE, CROSS OUT ALL THE LETTERS THAT APPEAR IN THE BOX FOUR TIMES. COMPLETE THE VERSE BY PLACING THE LETTERS THAT ARE LEFT OVER, AS THEY APPEAR, IN THE SPACES PROVIDED.

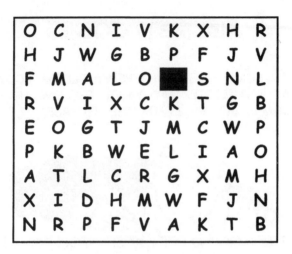

"WHEREFORE THEN SERVETH THE LAW? IT WAS ADDED BECAUSE OF TRANSGRESSIONS, TILL THE ___ ___ ___ ___ SHOULD COME TO WHOM THE PROMISE WAS MADE; AND IT WAS ORDAINED BY ANGELS IN THE HAND OF A MEDIATOR."

GALATIANS 3:19, KJV

SECRET CODES

TO SOLVE THE CODED VERSE BELOW, LOOK
AT EACH LETTER AND WRITE THE ONE THAT
COMES BEFORE IT IN THE ALPHABET.

"UIF QSPNJTFT XFSF TQPLFO UP
BCSBIBN BOE UP IJT TFFE. UIF
TDSJQUVSF EPFT OPU TBZ 'BOE UP
TFFET,' NFBOJOH NBOZ QFPQMF,
CVU 'BOE UP ZPVS TFFE,' NFBOJOH
POF QFSTPO, XIP JT DISJTU."

A B C D E F G H I J K L M N O P Q R S T
U V W X Y Z

"_____   _____

_____   _____   _____

_____   _____   _____

_____   _____.   _____

_____   _____   _____

_____   _____   _____ - _____

_____,   _____   _____

_____   _____,   _____

'_____   _____   _____

_____,   _____   _____

_____   _____,   _____

_____   _____."

GALATIANS 3:16

DOUBLE the FUN

UNSCRAMBLE THE UNDERLINED WORDS IN THE VERSES. ON THE NEXT PAGE, PLACE YOUR ANSWERS IN THE SPACES PROVIDED AND THEN COMPLETE THE CROSSWORD PUZZLE.

"THE LAW WAS <u>DAEDD</u> SO THAT THE <u>PERSATSS</u> MIGHT <u>REESNICA</u>. BUT WHERE SIN INCREASED, GRACE INCREASED ALL THE MORE, SO THAT, JUST AS SIN REIGNED IN DEATH, SO ALSO GRACE MIGHT REIGN THROUGH <u>GSETIRSUEHSNO</u> TO BRING <u>EAELRNT</u> LIFE THROUGH JESUS <u>IRSTHC</u> OUR LORD."

ROMANS 5:20-21

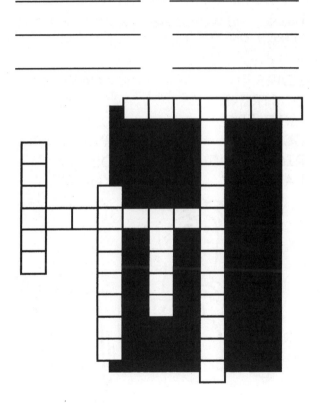

215

FILL in the BLANKS

USING THE WORDS BELOW, COMPLETE THE
VERSES ON THE NEXT PAGE.

LIARS
DOCTRINE
MOTHERS
GOOD
RIGHTEOUS
LAWFULLY

CONTRARY
SINNERS
DISOBEDIENT
MURDERERS
DEFILE
KNOW

"BUT WE ____ THAT THE LAW IS ____, IF A MAN USE IT _____; KNOWING THIS, THAT THE LAW IS NOT MADE FOR A _____ MAN, BUT FOR THE LAWLESS AND _____, FOR THE UNGODLY AND FOR _____, FOR UNHOLY AND PROFANE, FOR _____ OF FATHERS AND MURDERERS OF _____, FOR MANSLAY-ERS, FOR WHOREMONGERS, FOR THEM THAT _____ THEMSELVES WITH MANKIND, FOR MENSTEALERS, FOR _____, FOR PERJURED PER-SONS, AND IF THERE BE ANY OTHER THING THAT IS _____ TO SOUND _____."

1 TIMOTHY 1:8–10, KJV

FINISH THE VERSE

USE THE CODE CHART BELOW TO FINISH THE VERSE ON THE NEXT PAGE. (EXAMPLE: K=24)

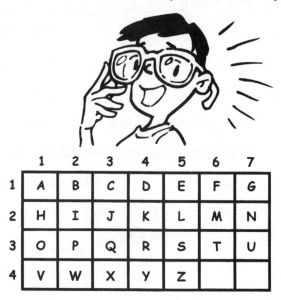

	1	2	3	4	5	6	7
1	A	B	C	D	E	F	G
2	H	I	J	K	L	M	N
3	O	P	Q	R	S	T	U
4	V	W	X	Y	Z		

"__ __ __ __ __ __ __ __ __ NO ONE
36 21 15 34 15 16 31 34 15

WILL   BE   __ __ __ __ __ __ __ __
14 15 13 25 11 34 15 14

__ __ __ __ __ __ __ __ __ IN HIS
34 22 17 21 36 15 31 37 35

SIGHT BY __ __ __ __ __ __ __ __ __
31 12 35 15 34 41 22 27 17

THE   LAW;   __ __ __ __ __ __,
34 11 36 21 15 34

THROUGH THE __ __ __ WE BECOME
25 11 42

__ __ __ __ __ __ __ __ __ OF
13 31 27 35 13 22 31 37 35

__ __ __."
35 22 27

ROMANS 3:20

SCRAMBLED VERSES

UNSCRAMBLE THE WORDS BELOW AND COMPLETE THE VERSE ON THE NEXT PAGE.

"RFOEEHTER, STJU SA NSI EDTEREN HET LODWR GTOHUHR EON NMA, DAN TEHAD RHUTGOH INS, NAD NI STHI AYW AHDET MEAC OT LAL NME, SCBEAEU LAL DISNEN—RFO FEORBE ETH WLA SWA VNGEI, ISN ASW NI EHT LWDRO."

"_____, _____
_____ ____ _____ ____ _____
_____ _____ ____ _____
_____ _____, ____ ____ _____
_____ _____, ___ _____
_____ _____ _____ _____
_____ _____ _____ ___ _____
_____ _____, ___ _____
_____ _____ — _____
_____ _____ ____ _____
_____ _____, ___ _____
_____ _____ _____ _____
_____."

ROMANS 5:12–13

DOUBLE the FUN

UNSCRAMBLE THE UNDERLINED WORDS IN EACH VERSE. ON THE NEXT PAGE, PLACE YOUR ANSWERS IN THE SPACES PROVIDED AND THEN COMPLETE THE CROSSWORD PUZZLE.

1. "WHAT SHALL WE SAY, ENHT? IS THE LAW SIN? NTECAYLIR NOT! INDEED I WOULD NOT HAVE KNOWN WHAT SIN WAS EXCEPT THROUGH THE LAW. FOR I WOULD NOT EHVA KNOWN WHAT NVCOTIGE REALLY WAS IF THE LAW HAD NOT SAID, 'DO NOT COVET.'"

ROMANS 7:7

2. "BUT SIN, IESZGNI THE OPPORTUNITY AFFORDED BY THE COMMANDMENT, PRODUCED IN ME EVERY KIND OF OOVCTSUE RESEID. FOR APART FROM LAW, NSI IS DEAD."

ROMANS 7:8

1. _____   _____

_____   _____

2. _____   _____

_____   _____

FILL in the BLANKS

USING THE WORDS BELOW, COMPLETE THE VERSES ON THE NEXT PAGE.

ORDAINED   DEATH
DIED   LAW
COMMANDMENT   SIN
LIFE   FOUND
ALIVE   WHEN

"FOR I WAS _____ WITHOUT THE _____ ONCE: BUT _____ THE _____ CAME, _____ REVIVED, AND I _____. AND THE COMMANDMENT, WHICH WAS _____ TO _____, I _____ TO BE UNTO _____."

ROMANS 7:9–10, KJV

SECRET CODES

TO SOLVE THE CODED VERSES BELOW, LOOK AT EACH LETTER AND WRITE THE ONE THAT COMES BEFORE IT IN THE ALPHABET.

"GPS TJO, TFJAJOH UIF PQQPSUVOJUZ BGGPSEFE CZ UIF DPNNBOEFNFOU, EFDFJWFE NF, BOE UISPVHI UIF DPNNBOEFNFOU QVU NF UP EFBUI. TP UIFO, UIF MBX JT IPMZ, BOE UIF DPNNBOEFNFOU JT IPMZ, SJHIUFPVT BOE HPPE."

A B C D E F G H I J K L M N O P Q R S T
U V W X Y Z

"_____ _____, _____

_____ _____ _____

_____ _____ _____ _____

_____,

_____ _____, _____

_____ _____ _____

_____ _____ _____

_____ _____ _____. _____

_____, _____ _____ _____

_____, _____ _____ _____

_____ _____

_____, _____

_____ _____."

ROMANS 7:11–12

227

SCRAMBLED CIRCLES

ON THE NEXT PAGE, UNSCRAMBLE THE WORDS IN THE LIST BELOW. THEN USE THE CIRCLED LETTERS TO COMPLETE THE VERSE.

1. EBRO

2. LTUTRYE

3. VCEEEDI

4. DGOO

5. NESMA

6. IFLE

1. _ _◯_
2. _ _ _◯_ _ _
3. _ _◯_ _ _ _
4. _◯_ _
5. ◯_ _ _ _
6. _ _ _◯

"THE OLD SYSTEM UNDER THE LAW OF MOSES WAS ONLY A ___ ___ ___ ___ ___ ___, A DIM PREVIEW OF THE GOOD THINGS TO COME, NOT THE GOOD THINGS THEMSELVES."

HEBREWS 10:1, NLT

CROSSWORD

GALATIANS 3:22–24

ACROSS

1. "BUT THE SCRIPTURE DECLARES THAT THE WHOLE WORLD IS A _____ OF SIN."
2. "SO THAT WHAT WAS _____."
3. "BEING GIVEN THROUGH FAITH IN _____ CHRIST."
4. "MIGHT BE GIVEN TO THOSE _____ BELIEVE."

DOWN

1. " BEFORE THIS FAITH CAME, WE WERE HELD _____ BY THE LAW."
2. "LOCKED UP UNTIL _____ SHOULD BE REVEALED."
3. "SO THE LAW WAS PUT IN _____ TO LEAD US TO CHRIST."
4. "THAT ___ MIGHT BE JUSTIFIED BY FAITH."

231

ASK YOURSELF

WHAT HAVE YOU LEARNED SO FAR? FIND OUT
BY ANSWERING THE QUESTIONS BELOW.

1. WHAT DOES THE SCRIPTURE SAY
   ABOUT THE WHOLE WORLD?

   GALATIANS 3:22–24

   _____

2. HOW IS THE PROMISE GIVEN?

   GALATIANS 3:22–24

   _____

3. WHO CAN RECEIVE THIS PROMISE?

   GALATIANS 3:22–24

   _____

4. WHAT HOLDS US PRISONER TO OUR SIN?

GALATIANS 3:22–24

_____

5. HOW LONG WOULD THE LAW KEEP US LOCKED UP?

GALATIANS 3:22–24

_____

6. WHY WAS THE LAW PUT IN CHARGE TO LEAD US TO CHRIST?

GALATIANS 3:22–24

_____

COLOR THE PICTURE

THE LAW IS POWERLESS...

THE LAW IS LIKE A MIRROR. IT CAN SHOW US THAT OUR FACES ARE DIRTY, BUT IT CAN'T WASH THEM FOR US.

THIS IS ALL GOD WANTED THE LAW TO DO. IT SHOWS US THAT WE ARE *DEAD IN OUR SINS* AND IN NEED OF *LIFE*, BUT IT IS POWERLESS TO DO ANYTHING OTHER THAN THAT.

THE LAW CANNOT GIVE LIFE—IF IT COULD, THEN WOULD THERE HAVE BEEN ANY NEED FOR JESUS TO COME? IF THE LAW COULD HAVE MADE ANYONE PERFECT OR GIVEN ANYONE LIFE, THEN JESUS' SACRIFICE FOR US WOULD HAVE BEEN FOR NOTHING.

ONLY JESUS CHRIST CAN GIVE LIFE!

DOUBLE the FUN

UNSCRAMBLE THE UNDERLINED WORDS IN EACH VERSE. ON THE NEXT PAGE, PLACE YOUR ANSWERS IN THE SPACES PROVIDED AND THEN COMPLETE THE CROSSWORD PUZZLE.

1. "THE MFORRE GAONTEULIR IS SET DSIAE BECAUSE IT WAS WEAK AND USELESS."

HEBREWS 7:18

2. "(FOR THE WLA MADE NOTHING EFTCRPE), AND A BTERTE HOPE IS DTEDOINRCU, BY WHICH WE WRDA NEAR TO GOD."

HEBREWS 7:19

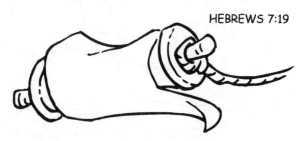

1. _____ _____
   _____
2. _____ _____
   _____
   _____

CROSS 'EM OUT

ON THE NEXT PAGE, CROSS OUT ALL THE
LETTERS THAT APPEAR IN THE BOX FOUR
TIMES. COMPLETE THE VERSE BY PLACING
THE LETTERS THAT ARE LEFT OVER, AS THEY
APPEAR, IN THE SPACES PROVIDED.

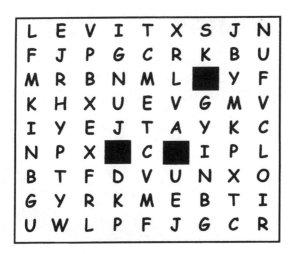

L	E	V	I	T	X	S	J	N
F	J	P	G	C	R	K	B	U
M	R	B	N	M	L	■	Y	F
K	H	X	U	E	V	G	M	V
I	Y	E	J	T	A	Y	K	C
N	P	X	■	C	■	I	P	L
B	T	F	D	V	U	N	X	O
G	Y	R	K	M	E	B	T	I
U	W	L	P	F	J	G	C	R

"THE OLD SYSTEM UNDER THE LAW OF MOSES WAS ONLY A ___ ___ ___ ___ ___ ___, A DIM PREVIEW OF THE GOOD THINGS TO COME, NOT THE GOOD THINGS THEMSELVES."

HEBREWS 10:1, NLT

FINISH the VERSE

USE THE CODE CHART BELOW TO FINISH THE
VERSE ON THE NEXT PAGE. (EXAMPLE: K=24)

	1	2	3	4	5	6	7
1	A	B	C	D	E	F	G
2	H	I	J	K	L	M	N
3	O	P	Q	R	S	T	U
4	V	W	X	Y	Z		

"FOR WHAT THE LAW WAS

___ ___ ___ ___ ___ ___ ___ ___ ___ TO DO IN
32 31 42 15 34 25 15 35 35

THAT IT WAS ___ ___ ___ ___ ___ ___ ___ ___
42 15 11 24 15 27 15 14

BY THE SINFUL ___ ___ ___ ___ ___ ___,
27 11 36 37 34 15

___ ___ ___ DID BY SENDING HIS OWN
17 31 14

___ ___ ___ IN THE LIKENESS OF
35 31 27

___ ___ ___ ___ ___ ___ MAN TO BE A SIN
35 22 27 16 37 25

___ ___ ___ ___ ___ ___ ___ ___. AND SO HE
31 16 16 15 34 22 27 17

CONDEMNED ___ ___ ___ IN SINFUL
35 22 27

MAN."

ROMANS 8:3

241

SCRAMBLED VERSES

UNSCRAMBLE THE WORDS BELOW AND COMPLETE THE VERSE ON THE NEXT PAGE.

"SI ETH WLA, ORHTEREFE, SPOOEDP OT HET SMRPIESO FO DGO? TOBALLYEUS OTN! RFO FI A WAL AHD NBEE EGNVI ATHT UCODL RPIMAT FELI, NHET NEGRTSEUHISOS LODUW AECTNYLIR AHVE CEOM YB ETH AWL."

"_____ _____ _____,

_____, _____

___ ___ _____

___ _____? _____

___! ___ ___ ___ ___

___ ___ _____

___ ___ ___

___, ___ _____-

___ ___ _____

___ ___ ___ ___ _____

___."

GALATIANS 3:21

243

SCRAMBLED CIRCLES

ON THE NEXT PAGE, UNSCRAMBLE THE WORDS IN THE LIST BELOW. THEN USE THE CIRCLED LETTERS TO COMPLETE THE VERSE.

1. ETJUIDISF

2. WLA

3. LILW

4. CIRTSH

5. UHTOHGR

1. _ _ _ _ _ ◯ _ _ _

2. _ ◯ _

3. _ ◯ _ _

4. _ _ _ _ _ ◯

5. _ ◯ _ _ _ _ _

"KNOW THAT A MAN IS NOT JUSTIFIED BY OBSERVING THE LAW, BUT BY ___ ___ ___ ___ ___ IN JESUS CHRIST."

GALATIANS 2:16

SECRET CODES

TO SOLVE THE CODED VERSES BELOW, LOOK
AT EACH LETTER AND WRITE THE ONE THAT
COMES BEFORE IT IN THE ALPHABET.

"CVU CFDBVTF PG IJT HSFBU MPWF

GPS VT, HPE, XIP JT SJDI JO NFSDZ,

NBEF   VT   BMJWF   XJUI   DISJTU

FWFO   XIFO   XF   XFSF   EFBE   JO

USBOTHSFTTJPOT—JU JT CZ HSBDF

ZPV IBWF CFFO TBWFE."

246

A B C D E F G H I J K L M N O P Q R S T
U V W X Y Z

"_____ _____ ____

_____ _____ _____

_____ ____, _____, _____

_____ _____ _____,

_____ _____ _____

_____ _____ _____

_____ ____ __ _____

____ _____ _

____ ____ _____ _____

____ _____ _____

_____."

EPHESIANS 2:4–5

247

ASK YOURSELF

WHAT HAVE YOU LEARNED SO FAR? FIND OUT
BY ANSWERING THE QUESTIONS BELOW.

1. WHAT HAS HAPPENED TO THE LAW
   FOR TODAY?

   HEBREWS 7:18–19

   _____

2. CAN A PERSON BE JUSTIFIED BY
   KEEPING THE LAW?

   GALATIANS 2:16

   _____

3. HOW THEN ARE WE JUSTIFIED?

   GALATIANS 2:16

   _____

4. DOES THE LAW HAVE THE ABILITY TO GIVE US LIFE?

ROMANS 7:10

_____

5. WHAT DOES THE LAW BRING?

ROMANS 7:10

_____

6. WHO MADE US ALIVE WITH CHRIST?

EPHESIANS 2:4–5

_____

COLOR THE PICTURE

CHRIST FULFILLED THE LAW

JESUS DID NOT COME TO ABOLISH THE LAW—HE CAME TO *FULFILL* IT. EVERY REQUIREMENT THAT THE LAW DEMANDED, JESUS MET, AND HE MET IT PERFECTLY. HE LIVED A COMPLETELY SINLESS LIFE; HE WALKED IN PERFECT LOVE.

HIS DEATH ON THE CROSS PAID IN FULL THE WAGES OF SIN FOR THE ENTIRE WORLD.

JESUS CHRIST DID IT ALL—FOR US!

GOD NAILED THE LAW TO THE CROSS; HE WAS COMPLETELY SATISFIED WITH THE SACRIFICE THAT HIS SON MADE ON OUR BEHALF.

IT IS GOD'S DESIRE THAT THE LAW REMAIN NAILED TO THAT CROSS!

251

CROSSWORD

ACROSS

1. "'DO NOT _____ THAT I HAVE COME.'"
2. "'TO _____ THE LAW OR THE PROPHETS.'"
3. "'I HAVE NOT COME TO ABOLISH _____.'"
4. "'BUT TO FULFILL _____.'"

DOWN

1. "'I TELL YOU THE TRUTH, UNTIL HEAVEN AND EARTH _____.'"
2. "'NOT THE SMALLEST _____, NOT THE LEAST STROKE OF A PEN.'"
3. "'WILL BY ANY _____ DISAPPEAR FROM THE LAW.'"
4. "'_____ EVERYTHING IS ACCOMPLISHED.'"

253

SCRAMBLED VERSES

UNSCRAMBLE THE WORDS BELOW AND COMPLETE THE VERSE ON THE NEXT PAGE.

"EH IDSA OT METH, 'HIST SI HATW I ODLT UYO IHELW I WSA LITSL TWIH UYO: IYVETGNHRE UTMS EB LLUFLDEIF AHTT SI TEWNIRT OATUB EM IN HET LWA FO OESSM, ETH SPRPHTEO DAN HET MASLPS.'"

254

"_____ _____ _____ _____,
'_____ _____ _____ _____
_____ _____ _____ _____
_____ _____ _____
_____: _____
_____ _____ _____
_____ _____ _____
_____ _____ _____ _____
_____ _____ _____,
_____ _____ _____
_____ _____.'"

LUKE 24:44

255

CROSS 'EM OUT

ON THE NEXT PAGE, CROSS OUT ALL THE
LETTERS THAT APPEAR IN THE BOX FOUR
TIMES. COMPLETE THE VERSE BY PLACING
THE LETTERS THAT ARE LEFT OVER, AS THEY
APPEAR, IN THE SPACES PROVIDED.

M	F	H	W	C	Y	N		J	Z
K	B	O	U	L	G	B		K	P
V	N	Y	A	W	M	█		D	F
C	W	J	K	B	V	A		N	Y
G	U	R	D	H	Z	D		W	G
O	D	L	N	F	I	C		E	L
Z	M	█	H	Y	█	V		F	U
J	S	V	A	C	O	H		J	O
U	K	B	Z	G	L	T		M	A

"FOR   WE   DO   NOT   HAVE   A   HIGH
___ ___ ___ ___ ___ ___ WHO IS UNABLE
TO SYMPATHIZE WITH OUR WEAKNESSES."

HEBREWS 4:15, ESV

257

FINISH THE VERSE

USE THE CODE CHART BELOW TO FINISH THE VERSE ON THE NEXT PAGE. (EXAMPLE: K=24)

	1	2	3	4	5	6	7
1	A	B	C	D	E	F	G
2	H	I	J	K	L	M	N
3	O	P	Q	R	S	T	U
4	V	W	X	Y	Z		

"FOR THE __ __ __ __ __ OF __ __ __
         42 11 17 15 35   35 22 27

IS __ __ __ __ __,   BUT   THE
   14 15 11 36 21

__ __ __ __ OF __ __ __ IS
17 22 16 36   17 31 14

__ __ __ __ __ __ __   __ __ __ __
15 36 15 34 27 11 25   25 22 16 15

IN   CHRIST __ __ __ __ __   OUR
            23 15 35 37 35

__ __ __ __."
25 31 34 14

ROMANS 6:23

259

SCRAMBLED CIRCLES

ON THE NEXT PAGE, UNSCRAMBLE THE WORDS
IN THE LIST BELOW. THEN USE THE CIRCLED
LETTERS TO COMPLETE THE VERSE.

1. NEETRLA

2. FITG

3. UTWIHTO

4. NBELAU

5. RESIPT

6. NSI

7. EWASG

1. _ _ _ _ _ ⃝ _

2. _ _ _ ⃝

3. _ _ _ _ ⃝ _ _

4. _ ⃝ _ _ _ _

5. _ _ ⃝ _ _ _

6. _ _ ⃝

7. _ _ ⃝ _ _

"HE IS THE _ _ _ _ _ _ _
SACRIFICE FOR OUR SINS, AND NOT
ONLY FOR OURS BUT ALSO FOR THE SINS
OF THE WHOLE WORLD."

1 JOHN 2:2

FILL in the BLANKS

USING THE WORDS BELOW, COMPLETE THE
VERSES ON THE NEXT PAGE.

CUT   GOD
CROSS   CANCELED
CHARGES   NAILING
ALIVE   SINFUL
FORGAVE   DEAD

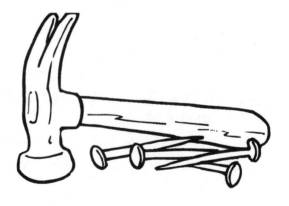

"YOU WERE ____ BECAUSE OF YOUR SINS AND BECAUSE YOUR _____ NATURE WAS NOT YET ___ AWAY. THEN ___ MADE YOU _____ WITH CHRIST, FOR HE _____ ALL OUR SINS. HE _____ THE RECORD OF THE _____ AGAINST US AND TOOK IT AWAY BY _____ IT TO THE _____."

COLOSSIANS 2:13–14, NLT

DOUBLE the FUN

UNSCRAMBLE THE UNDERLINED WORDS IN EACH VERSE. ON THE NEXT PAGE, PLACE YOUR ANSWERS IN THE SPACES PROVIDED AND THEN COMPLETE THE CROSSWORD PUZZLE.

1. "FOR WHAT THE LAW WAS <u>LOWESEPRS</u> TO DO IN THAT IT WAS <u>NKEWEDEA</u> BY THE SINFUL NATURE, GOD DID BY <u>NNSDGIE</u> HIS OWN SON IN THE LIKENESS OF <u>NLUSFI</u> MAN TO BE A SIN OFFERING."

ROMANS 8:3

2. "AND SO HE <u>MODNDCEEN</u> SIN IN SINFUL MAN, IN ORDER THAT THE RIGHTEOUS REQUIREMENTS OF THE LAW MIGHT BE FULLY MET IN US, WHO <u>OD</u> NOT <u>ILEV</u> ACCORDING TO THE SINFUL NATURE BUT ACCORDING TO THE <u>IRISTP</u>."

ROMANS 8:3-4

1. _____   _____

_____   _____

2. _____   _____

_____   _____

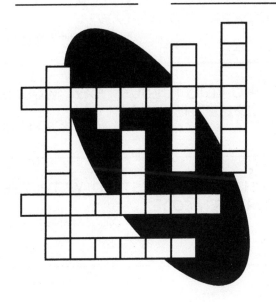

ASK YOURSELF

WHAT HAVE YOU LEARNED SO FAR? FIND OUT
BY ANSWERING THE QUESTIONS BELOW.

1. WHAT DID CHRIST COME TO DO
CONCERNING THE LAW?

MATTHEW 5:17–18

_____

2. WHO DID JESUS SAY WOULD
FULFILL THE LAW?

MATTHEW 5:17–18

_____

3. WHAT DID CHRIST DO WITH THE
WRITTEN CODE?

COLOSSIANS 2:13–14

_____

4. ONCE THE LAW WAS CANCELLED, WHAT DID JESUS DO WITH IT?

COLOSSIANS 2:13–14

_____

5. THEREFORE, WHERE SHOULD THE LAW REMAIN?

COLOSSIANS 2:14

_____

6. SINCE JESUS FULFILLED THE LAW, DOES IT MAKE ANY SENSE FOR US TO TRY TO FULFILL IT?

GALATIANS 3:1–3

_____

COLOR *THE* PICTURE

CHRIST SET US FREE FROM THE LAW

WE WERE BORN INTO THIS WORLD AS SLAVES TO SIN. WE WERE BORN SPIRITUALLY *DEAD*.

BY THE LAW, WE WERE HELD PRISONER TO OUR SINFULNESS. FOR US TO BE SET FREE, A PRICE HAD TO BE PAID. THE PRICE THAT THE LAW REQUIRED WAS THE *PRECIOUS BLOOD OF JESUS*—NOTHING ELSE WOULD DO.

AT THE RIGHT TIME, GOD SENT HIS SON, JESUS, INTO THE WORLD TO PAY THE PRICE THAT THE LAW DEMANDED. JESUS REDEEMED US FROM THE LAW OF SIN AND DEATH.

HE DID THIS, NOT TO KEEP US AS SLAVES, BUT TO SET US FREE—TO MAKE US HIS SONS AND DAUGHTERS AND TO GIVE US THE FULL RIGHT TO BECOME *CHILDREN OF GOD*.

FILL in the BLANKS

USING THE WORDS BELOW, COMPLETE THE VERSE ON THE NEXT PAGE.

ONE

CURSED

TREE

MADE

LAW

WRITTEN

CURSE

HANGETH

CHRIST

REDEEMED

"_____ HATH _____ US FROM THE CURSE
OF THE ___, BEING ____ A _____ FOR US: FOR
IT IS _____, _____ IS EVERY ___ THAT
_____ ON A ____."

GALATIANS 3:13, KJV

271

FINISH THE VERSE

USE THE CODE CHART BELOW TO FINISH THE
VERSES ON THE NEXT PAGE. (EXAMPLE: K=24)

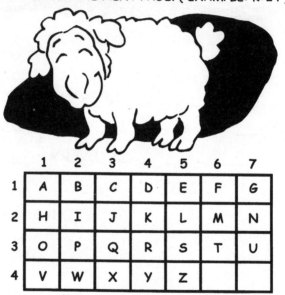

	1	2	3	4	5	6	7
1	A	B	C	D	E	F	G
2	H	I	J	K	L	M	N
3	O	P	Q	R	S	T	U
4	V	W	X	Y	Z		

"FOR YOU ___ ___ ___ ___ THAT
        24 27 31 42

IT WAS NOT WITH

___ ___ ___ ___ ___ ___ ___ ___ ___
32 15 34 22 35 21 11 12 25 15

THINGS SUCH AS ___ ___ ___ ___ ___ ___
               35 22 25 41 15 34

OR ___ ___ ___ ___ THAT YOU WERE
   17 31 25 14

REDEEMED FROM THE ___ ___ ___ ___ ___
                  15 26 32 36 44

WAY OF ___ ___ ___ ___ HANDED DOWN
       25 22 16 15

TO YOU FROM YOUR

___ ___ ___ ___ ___ ___ ___ ___ ___ ___,
16 31 34 15 16 11 36 21 15 34 35

BUT WITH THE ___ ___ ___ ___ ___ ___ ___
             32 34 15 13 22 31 37 35

BLOOD OF CHRIST, A ___ ___ ___ ___
                   25 11 26 12

WITHOUT BLEMISH OR

___ ___ ___ ___ ___ ___."
14 15 16 15 13 36

1 PETER 1:18–19

273

DOUBLE *the* FUN

UNSCRAMBLE THE UNDERLINED WORDS IN EACH VERSE. ON THE NEXT PAGE, PLACE YOUR ANSWERS IN THE SPACES PROVIDED AND THEN COMPLETE THE CROSSWORD PUZZLE.

1. "'THEN YOU WILL KNOW THE TRTHU, AND THE TRUTH WILL SET YOU EFER.'"

   JOHN 8:32

2. "THEY ANSWERED HIM, 'WE ARE ABRAHAM'S DCESNNSAEDT AND HAVE NEVER BEEN SLAVES OF NOENAY. HOW CAN YOU SAY THAT WE SHALL BE SET FREE?'"

   JOHN 8:33

3. "JESUS PRLDIEE, 'I TELL YOU THE TRUTH, YVNEOERE WHO SINS IS A SLAVE TO SIN.'"

   JOHN 8:34

274

1. _____   _____

2. _____   _____

3. _____   _____

SCRAMBLED VERSES

UNSCRAMBLE THE WORDS BELOW AND
COMPLETE THE VERSE ON THE NEXT PAGE.

"TBU ETH RTEUICSPR RCEDLASE ATTH
HET OELWH DOWLR SI A NPIREROS
FO NSI, OS HTTA AWTH SWA
MSEDRPOI, NIBEG VGNIE RGUHOHT
AHFTI NI UESJS IHRCTS, GITMH EB
EINVG OT SEHOT OWH ELEBIVE."

"_____ _____ _____

_____ _____ _____

_____ _____ _____ _

_____ ___ _____,

_____ _____ _____ _____

_____, _____

_____ _____

_____ ____ _____

_____, _____ ___

_____ _____ _____

_____ _____."

GALATIANS 3:22

CROSSWORD

ACROSS

1. "HE DID NOT ENTER BY _____ OF THE BLOOD OF GOATS AND CALVES."
2. "BUT HE _____ THE MOST HOLY PLACE ONCE FOR ALL."
3. "BY HIS OWN _____."
4. "_____ OBTAINED ETERNAL REDEMPTION."

DOWN

1. "HOW MUCH _____, THEN, WILL THE BLOOD OF CHRIST."
2. "WHO THROUGH THE _____ SPIRIT OFFERED HIMSELF UNBLEMISHED TO GOD."
3. "CLEANSE OUR CONSCIENCES FROM ACTS THAT LEAD TO _____."
4. "SO THAT WE MAY SERVE THE LIVING _____!"

279

CROSS 'EM OUT

ON THE NEXT PAGE, CROSS OUT ALL THE
LETTERS THAT APPEAR IN THE BOX FOUR
TIMES. COMPLETE THE VERSE BY PLACING
THE LETTERS THAT ARE LEFT OVER, AS THEY
APPEAR, IN THE SPACES PROVIDED.

```
P  M  E  W  J  K  B  L  V
F  B  O  A  X  G  P  O  E
K  G  Y  L  D  N  M  U  C
D  V  J  U  ■  V  Y  F  N
N  W  ■  H  P  W  A  D  X
X  A  F  O  Y  R  K  G  J
E  M  Y  ■  W  X  E  U  B
L  I  P  N  A  O  L  S  M
T  U  B  G  V  J  D  K  F
```

"THERE IS THEREFORE NOW NO CON-
DEMNATION TO THEM WHICH ARE IN
___ ___ ___ ___ ___ ___ JESUS."
ROMANS 8:1, KJV

SECRET CODES

TO SOLVE THE CODED VERSES BELOW, LOOK
AT EACH LETTER AND WRITE THE ONE THAT
COMES BEFORE IT IN THE ALPHABET.

"CVU XIFO UIF UJNF IBE GVMMZ
DPNF, HPE TFOU IJT TPO, CPSO PG B
XPNBO, CPSO VOEFS MBX, UP SFEFFN
UIPTF VOEFS MBX, UIBU XF NJHIU
SFDFJWF UIF GVMM SJHIUT PG
TPOT."

282

A B C D E F G H I J K L M N O P Q R S T
U V W X Y Z

"_____ _____ _____

_____ _____ _____

_____, _____ _____

_____ _____, _____ _____

_____ _____, _____

_____ _____, _____

_____ _____

_____ _____, _____

_____ _____ _____

_____ _____ _____

_____ _____."

GALATIANS 4:4–5

283

SCRAMBLED CIRCLES

ON THE NEXT PAGE, UNSCRAMBLE THE WORDS
IN THE LIST BELOW. THEN USE THE CIRCLED
LETTERS TO COMPLETE THE VERSE.

1. RETSAH
2. ALSLC
3. NTSAD
4. EEREICV
5. REFE
6. PITRIS
7. ULYLF

284

1. _ _ _ _ _ ◯

2. _ _ ◯ _ _

3. _ _ ◯ _ _

4. _ _ _ _ _ ◯ _

5. _ _ ◯ _

6. _ _ _ ◯ _ _

7. _ _ _ _ ◯

"IT IS FOR FREEDOM THAT CHRIST HAS SET US FREE. STAND FIRM, THEN, AND DO NOT LET YOURSELVES BE BURDENED AGAIN BY A YOKE OF _ _ _ _ _ _ _."

GALATIANS 5:1

285

ASK YOURSELF

WHAT HAVE YOU LEARNED SO FAR? FIND OUT
BY ANSWERING THE QUESTIONS BELOW.

1. WHAT DID JESUS REDEEM US
   FROM?

   GALATIANS 3:13–14

   _____

2. HOW DID HE REDEEM US?

   GALATIANS 3:13–14

   _____

3. HOW DID CHRIST BECOME A
   "CURSE"?

   GALATIANS 3:13–14

   _____

4. WHEN WE PUT OUR FAITH IN JESUS, WHAT DO WE RECEIVE?

GALATIANS 3:13–14

_____

5. IS THERE ANY CONDEMNATION FOR THOSE WHO ARE IN CHRIST?

ROMANS 8:1–2

_____

6. WHAT HAS THE SPIRIT OF LIFE SET US FREE FROM?

ROMANS 8:1–2

_____

COLOR *the* PICTURE

HOPELESSNESS UNDER THE LAW

THE LAW IS TOUGH TO LIVE BY—IN FACT, IT'S *IMPOSSIBLE* TO LIVE BY!

THE LAW REQUIRES US TO BE *ABSOLUTELY* PERFECT, TO BE *ABSOLUTELY* OBEDIENT TO ALL ITS REGULATIONS. THE LAW HAS NO MERCY. IF WE BREAK JUST ONE OF THE COMMANDMENTS, THEN WE ARE GUILTY OF BREAKING THEM ALL.

THE VERY LAW THAT DEMANDED PERFECTION IS ACTUALLY RESPONSIBLE FOR STIRRING UP SIN IN US. SO LIVING UNDER THE LAW IS A NO-WIN SITUATION. THERE IS *NO HOPE* IN THE LAW!

THE LAW NOT ONLY LEADS US TO CHRIST, IT SHOWS US HOW DESPERATELY WE NEED HIM TO LIVE.

CROSS 'EM OUT

ON THE NEXT PAGE, CROSS OUT ALL THE
LETTERS THAT APPEAR IN THE BOX FOUR
TIMES. COMPLETE THE VERSE BY PLACING
THE LETTERS THAT ARE LEFT OVER, AS THEY
APPEAR, IN THE SPACES PROVIDED.

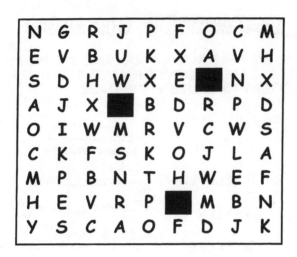

N	G	R	J	P	F	O	C	M
E	V	B	U	K	X	A	V	H
S	D	H	W	X	E	■	N	X
A	J	X	■	B	D	R	P	D
O	I	W	M	R	V	C	W	S
C	K	F	S	K	O	J	L	A
M	P	B	N	T	H	W	E	F
H	E	V	R	P	■	M	B	N
Y	S	C	A	O	F	D	J	K

"FOR THE PERSON WHO KEEPS ALL OF THE LAWS
EXCEPT ONE IS AS ___ ___ ___ ___ ___ ___
AS A PERSON WHO HAS BROKEN ALL OF GOD'S
LAWS.'

JAMES 2:10, NLT

SCRAMBLED CIRCLES

ON THE NEXT PAGE, UNSCRAMBLE THE WORDS IN THE LIST BELOW. THEN USE THE CIRCLED LETTERS TO COMPLETE THE VERSE.

1. EFCA

2. ELUFLSNS

3. YELR

4. PKSEE

5. RTENTIW

6. TDNSA

1. _ _ 〇 _

2. _ 〇 _ _ _ _ _ _

3. 〇 _ _ _

4. _ _ _ _ 〇

5. _ _ _ _ _ 〇 _

6. _ _ _ 〇

"ALL WHO RELY ON OBSERVING THE LAW ARE UNDER A CURSE, FOR IT IS WRITTEN: '_ _ _ _ _ _ IS EVERYONE WHO DOES NOT CONTINUE TO DO EVERYTHING WRITTEN IN THE BOOK OF THE LAW.'"

GALATIANS 3:10

DOUBLE *the* FUN

UNSCRAMBLE THE UNDERLINED WORDS IN EACH VERSE. ON THE NEXT PAGE, PLACE YOUR ANSWERS IN THE SPACES PROVIDED AND THEN COMPLETE THE CROSSWORD PUZZLE.

1. "'YOU HAVE HEARD THAT IT WAS SAID TO THE <u>PLPEOE</u> LONG AGO, "DO NOT <u>DUMRRE</u>, AND ANYONE WHO MURDERS WILL BE <u>EBSJTUC</u> TO JUDGMENT."'"

   MATTHEW 5:21

2. "'BUT I TELL YOU THAT <u>NNYAEO</u> WHO IS ANGRY WITH HIS BROTHER WILL BE SUBJECT TO JUDGMENT. AGAIN, ANYONE WHO SAYS TO HIS BROTHER, "RACA," IS ANSWERABLE TO THE <u>DNSIREAHN</u>. BUT ANYONE WHO SAYS, "YOU FOOL!" WILL BE IN <u>EANRGD</u> OF THE FIRE OF HELL.'"

   MATTHEW 5:22

1. _____ _____

   _____

2. _____ _____

   _____

FILL in the BLANKS

USING THE WORDS BELOW, COMPLETE THE VERSE ON THE NEXT PAGE.

WITHIN

CUP

OUTSIDE

FULL

HYPOCRITES

SCRIBES

PLATTER

WOE

CLEAN

EXCESS

"___ UNTO YOU, _____ AND PHARISEES,

_____! FOR YE MAKE _____ THE _____

OF THE ___ AND OF THE _____, BUT _____

THEY ARE ____ OF EXTORTION AND _____."

MATTHEW 23:25, KJV

CROSSWORD

COLOSSIANS 2:20–22

ACROSS

1. "SINCE YOU DIED WITH CHRIST TO THE BASIC _____ OF THIS WORLD."
2. "WHY, AS THOUGH YOU STILL _____ TO IT."
3. "DO YOU SUBMIT TO ITS _____."
4. "'DO NOT HANDLE! DO NOT TASTE! DO NOT _____!'?"

DOWN

1. "THESE ARE ALL _____."
2. "TO _____ WITH USE."
3. "BECAUSE THEY _____ BASED."
4. "ON HUMAN COMMANDS AND _____."

ASK YOURSELF

WHAT HAVE YOU LEARNED SO FAR? FIND OUT
BY ANSWERING THE QUESTIONS BELOW.

1. HOW MUCH OF THE LAW MUST BE
   BROKEN   TO   BE   GUILTY   OF
   BREAKING IT ALL?

   JAMES 2:10

   _____

2. HOW MUCH MUST BE KEPT TO OBEY
   IT ?

   JAMES 2:10

   _____

3. WHAT IS THE STING OF DEATH?

   1 CORINTHIANS 15:56

   _____

4. WHAT IS THE POWER OF SIN?

1 CORINTHIANS 15:56

_____

5. AS CHILDREN OF GOD, DO WE BELONG TO THE WORLD?

COLOSSIANS 2:20–23

_____

6. TO WHOM DO WE BELONG?

COLOSSIANS 2:20–23

_____

COLOR THE PICTURE

THE REAL PROBLEM WITH THE LAW

THE REAL PROBLEM WITH THE LAW IS. . .YOU AND ME!

THE LAW REQUIRES US TO PERFORM, TO LIVE UP TO ITS STANDARDS. BUT BECAUSE SIN LIVES IN OUR FLESH, WE CANNOT LIVE UP TO THE LAW. WE CANNOT FREE OURSELVES FROM THE POWER OF SIN NO MATTER HOW HARD WE TRY OR HOW MUCH WE WANT TO DO GOOD. WE WILL *ALWAYS* FALL SHORT.

THE CHRISTIAN *LIFE* IS ALL ABOUT JESUS CHRIST AND NOT ABOUT US. AS LONG AS WE TRY TO LIVE UNDER THE LAW, WE MISS OUT ON THE EXPERIENCE OF JESUS LIVING *HIS LIFE* THROUGH US.

WE CAN'T DO IT—BUT *HE* CAN!

SECRET CODES

TO SOLVE THE CODED VERSES BELOW, LOOK
AT EACH LETTER AND WRITE THE ONE THAT
COMES BEFORE IT IN THE ALPHABET.

"GPS JG UIFSF IBE CFFO OPUIJOH
XSPOH XJUI UIBU GJSTU
DPWFOBOU, OP QMBDF XPVME IBWF
CFFO TPVHIU GPS BOPUIFS. CVU HPE
GPVOE GBVMU XJUI UIF QFPQMF."

A B C D E F G H I J K L M N O P Q R S T
U V W X Y Z

"_____ ____ _____ ____ _____

_____ _____ _____

_____ ____ ____ _____

_____, ___ ____ _____

_____ ____ ____ _____

_____ ____ _____.

____ ____ _____

_____ ____ ____ ____

_____."

HEBREWS 8:7–8

SCRAMBLED VERSES

UNSCRAMBLE THE WORDS BELOW AND COMPLETE THE VERSES ON THE NEXT PAGE.

"EW ONWK TATH HET AWL SI TRPAIISUL; TUB I MA PTLUIUAISNR, LODS SA A VSLEA OT ISN. I OD TON NSDNRDUETA AWTH I OD. RFO TAHW I NWTA OT OD I OD OTN OD, UBT WTAH I TEHA I OD. DAN FI I OD ATHW I OD ONT TANW OT OD, I EARGE ATTH ETH LWA SI ODOG. SA TI SI, TI SI ON GLEORN I EYFSML HWO OD TI, TBU TI SI NSI VGIILN NI EM."

"＿＿ ＿＿＿ ＿＿＿ ＿＿＿
＿＿＿ ＿＿ ＿＿ ＿＿＿＿; ＿ ＿＿＿
＿ ＿＿ ＿＿＿＿＿＿,
＿＿＿ ＿＿＿ ＿＿ ＿＿ ＿＿＿
＿＿ ＿＿＿ ＿. ＿ ＿＿ ＿＿ ＿＿＿
＿＿＿＿ ＿＿＿ ＿＿
＿. ＿＿ ＿＿＿ ＿＿ ＿ ＿＿
＿＿ ＿＿ ＿＿ ＿＿ ＿,
＿＿＿ ＿＿＿ ＿＿ ＿＿＿ ＿＿
＿＿. ＿＿＿ ＿＿ ＿＿ ＿＿＿
＿＿＿ ＿＿ ＿＿ ＿＿＿ ＿＿
＿＿ ＿＿, ＿＿ ＿＿＿ ＿＿＿
＿＿ ＿＿＿ ＿＿ ＿＿ ＿＿＿.
＿＿ ＿＿ ＿＿ ＿, ＿＿ ＿＿ ＿＿
＿＿＿＿ ＿＿ ＿＿＿
＿＿ ＿＿, ＿＿＿ ＿＿ ＿＿ ＿"
＿＿ ＿＿ ＿＿＿＿ ＿＿ ＿＿."

ROMANS 7:14–17

307

FINISH THE VERSE

USE THE CODE CHART BELOW TO FINISH THE
VERSE ON THE NEXT PAGE. (EXAMPLE: K=24)

	1	2	3	4	5	6	7
1	A	B	C	D	E	F	G
2	H	I	J	K	L	M	N
3	O	P	Q	R	S	T	U
4	V	W	X	Y	Z		

"I HAVE BEEN __ __ __ __ __ __ __ __ __
13 34 37 13 22 16 22 15 14

WITH __ __ __ __ __ __ AND I NO
13 21 34 22 35 36

__ __ __ __ __ __ LIVE, BUT CHRIST
25 31 27 17 15 34

__ __ __ __ __ IN ME. THE LIFE I
25 22 41 15 35

__ __ __ __ IN THE __ __ __ __, I
25 22 41 15   12 31 14 44

LIVE BY __ __ __ __ __ IN THE
16 11 22 36 21

__ __ __ OF GOD, WHO __ __ __ __ __
35 31 27   25 31 41 15 14

ME AND GAVE __ __ __ __ __ __ __
21 22 26 35 15 25 16

FOR ME."

GALATIANS 2:20

309

ASK YOURSELF

WHAT HAVE YOU LEARNED SO FAR? FIND OUT
BY ANSWERING THE QUESTIONS BELOW.

1. WHEN WE ARE LIVING UNDER THE
   LAW, CAN WE UNDERSTAND WHY
   WE DO WHAT WE DO?
   ROMANS 7:15–24

   _____

2. UNDER THE LAW, ARE WE ABLE TO
   DO GOOD?
   ROMANS 7:15–24

   _____

3. WHAT DO WE END UP DOING?
   ROMANS 7:15–24

   _____

4. HOW MANY TIMES ARE THE WORDS "ME, MYSELF, AND I" USED IN THIS PASSAGE?

ROMANS 7:15–24

_____

5. UNDER THE LAW, WHO IS OUR FOCUS ON?

ROMANS 7:15–24

_____

6. IF WE ARE CRUCIFIED IN CHRIST, WHO LIVES IN US?

GALATIANS 2:19–20

_____

COLOR THE PICTURE

YOU CAN'T MIX LAW AND GRACE

YOU CAN'T MIX LAW AND GRACE. LAW IS OUR OWN SELF-EFFORT, WHILE GRACE IS CHRIST AND HIS FINISHED WORK ON THE CROSS—IT IS *HIM* LIVING HIS LIFE THROUGH US.

HAVE YOU EVER TRIED TO MIX OIL WITH WATER? THEY DON'T BLEND TOGETHER, NO MATTER HOW MUCH YOU TRY. SO IT IS WITH LAW AND GRACE—NO MATTER HOW HARD YOU MAY TRY, YOU'LL NEVER MAKE THEM BLEND. YOU'LL ONLY END UP FRUSTRATED AND ANGRY.

GRACE *ALONE* SAVED US AND IT WILL KEEP US GOING IN OUR CHRISTIAN LIFE. WE DO THIS BY DEPENDING ON JESUS, BELIEVING BY FAITH THAT WITH ALL OUR MISTAKES AND SIN, HE CONTINUES TO LOVE US AND *ACCEPT* US TOTALLY!

CROSSWORD

ACROSS

1. "YOU FOOLISH GALATIANS! WHO HAS
_____ YOU?"
2. "_____ YOUR VERY EYES."
3. "JESUS _____ WAS CLEARLY
PORTRAYED AS CRUCIFIED."
4. "I WOULD LIKE TO _____ JUST ONE
THING FROM YOU."

DOWN

1. "DID YOU RECEIVE THE SPIRIT BY
_____ THE LAW."
2. "OR BY _____ WHAT YOU
HEARD?"
3. "ARE YOU SO FOOLISH? AFTER
_____ WITH THE SPIRIT."
4. "ARE YOU NOW TRYING TO ATTAIN YOUR
GOAL BY _____ EFFORT?"

315

FILL in the BLANKS

USING THE WORDS BELOW, COMPLETE THE
VERSES ON THE NEXT PAGE.

GOOD   MERCY
FOLLOWING   PRETENDS
GOD   NEWS
SHOCKED   TWIST
AWAY   FOOLED

"I AM _____ THAT YOU ARE TURNING ___ SO SOON FROM ___, WHO CALLED YOU TO HIMSELF THROUGH THE LOVING _____ OF CHRIST. YOU ARE _____ A DIFFERENT WAY THAT _____ TO BE THE ___ NEWS BUT IS NOT THE GOOD ___ AT ALL. YOU ARE BEING _____ BY THOSE WHO DELIBERATELY _____ THE TRUTH CONCERNING CHRIST."

GALATIANS 1:6–7, NLT

CROSS 'EM OUT

ON THE NEXT PAGE, CROSS OUT ALL THE
LETTERS THAT APPEAR IN THE BOX FOUR
TIMES. COMPLETE THE VERSE BY PLACING
THE LETTERS THAT ARE LEFT OVER, AS THEY
APPEAR, IN THE SPACES PROVIDED.

```
F Z H C I N M E J
M B Q L V A T G P
W U G P J V D U B
C E I F U B V F Z
Z V A N D Q N O T
I D L R T G U H M
G P J N K I C P A
Q Z T H B F E J L
A E L D Q M S H C
```

"AND IF BY GRACE, THEN IS IT NO MORE OF

___ ___ ___ ___ ___: OTHERWISE GRACE IS

NO MORE GRACE."

ROMANS 11:6, KJV

ASK YOURSELF

WHAT HAVE YOU LEARNED SO FAR? FIND OUT BY ANSWERING THE QUESTIONS BELOW.

1. HOW ARE WE SAVED?

ROMANS 11:6

_____

2. IF YOU TRY TO LIVE BY THE LAW AND BY GRACE, WHAT HAPPENS TO GRACE?

ROMANS 11:6

_____

3. WHAT VALUE DOES GRACE HAVE IF WE TRY BY OUR OWN EFFORT TO FIND SALVATION?

ROMANS 11:6

_____

4. ARE YOU TRYING TO LIVE AS A CHRISTIAN BY YOUR OWN SELF-EFFORT?

_____

5. AGAIN, WHAT IS THE PURPOSE OF THE LAW?

_____

6. IF YOU ARE A CHRISTIAN, WHERE DOES CHRIST LIVE?

_____

COLOR the PICTURE

THE GRACE OF GOD

THE GRACE OF GOD IS NOT SOMETHING WE CAN EASILY DEFINE—IT'S SOMETHING WE *EXPERIENCE*.

GRACE IS THE VERY NATURE OF GOD. TRYING TO DEFINE GRACE IS LIKE TRYING TO DEFINE GOD.

UNDERSTANDING THIS GRACE IS NOT EASY. WE ALWAYS THINK THAT WITH OTHER PEOPLE WE HAVE TO DO SOMETHING OR BEHAVE IN A CERTAIN WAY TO RECEIVE THEIR LOVE AND ACCEPTANCE. WHY NOT WITH GOD?

WE CAN PRAISE GOD THAT HE IS NOT LIKE US!

GRACE IS GOD'S *GIFT* TO US, A GIFT THAT WE DO NOT NEED TO EARN. WITH GOD, WE NEED ONLY *TO BE OURSELVES!*

FINISH THE VERSE

USE THE CODE CHART BELOW TO FINISH THE
VERSES ON THE NEXT PAGE. (EXAMPLE: K=24)

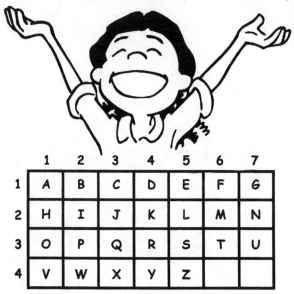

	1	2	3	4	5	6	7
1	A	B	C	D	E	F	G
2	H	I	J	K	L	M	N
3	O	P	Q	R	S	T	U
4	V	W	X	Y	Z		

"_____, SINCE WE
36 21 15 34 15 16 31 34 15

HAVE BEEN _____
23 3 7 35 36 22 16 22 15 14

THROUGH FAITH, WE HAVE

_____ WITH GOD THROUGH
32 15 11 13 15

OUR _____ JESUS CHRIST,
25 31 34 14

THROUGH WHOM WE HAVE

_____ _____
17 11 22 27 15 14   11 13 13 15 35 35

BY FAITH INTO THIS _____
17 34 11 13 15

IN WHICH WE NOW STAND. AND WE

_____ IN THE
34 15 23 31 22 13 15

_____ OF THE _____
21 31 32 15   17 25 31 34 44

OF GOD."

ROMANS 5:1–2

325

DOUBLE the FUN

UNSCRAMBLE THE UNDERLINED WORDS IN THE VERSES. ON THE NEXT PAGE, PLACE YOUR ANSWERS IN THE SPACES PROVIDED AND THEN COMPLETE THE CROSSWORD PUZZLE.

"FOR IT IS BY CAGER YOU HAVE NEBE VADES, THROUGH IHAFT — AND THIS NOT FROM SOVERYUESL, IT IS THE FITG OF GOD — NOT BY RSOWK, SO THAT NO ONE CAN ABTOS."

EPHESIANS 2:8–9

327

SECRET CODES

TO SOLVE THE CODED VERSES BELOW, LOOK AT EACH LETTER AND WRITE THE ONE THAT COMES BEFORE IT IN THE ALPHABET.

"CVU CFDBVTF PG IJT HSFBU MPWF
GPS VT, HPE, XIP JT SJDI JO NFSDZ,
NBEF VT BMJWF XJUI DISJTU
FWFO XIFO XF XFSF EFBE JO
USBOTHSFTTJPOT — JU JT CZ HSBDF
ZPV IBWF CFFO TBWFE."

328

ABCDEFGHIJKLMNOPQRST
UVWXYZ

"_____ _____ _____

_____ _____ _____

_____ _____, _____, _____

_____ _____ _____ _____,

_____ _____ _____

_____ _____ _____

_____ _____ _____

_____ _____

_ _____ _____ _____ _____

_____ _____ _____

_____."

EPHESIANS 2:4–5

329

SCRAMBLED VERSES

UNSCRAMBLE THE WORDS BELOW AND COMPLETE THE VERSES ON THE NEXT PAGE.

"NI IMH EW VEAH TERDPONIME HUHTOGR SHI ODOLB, ETH GESEIOFVSNR FO NSIS, NI NRCOAEADCC TIHW HTE EICSHR FO D'GSO EAGRC TATH EH AHDVSELI NO SU TIHW LAL OSWIDM DNA NDRUTIEAGNSND."

"_____ _____ _____ _____

_____ _____

_____ _____, _____

_____ ___ __ _____,

_____ _____

_____ __ _____ _____

_____ _____ _____

_____ ____ _____

_____ _____ _____

_____ _____ _____

_____ . "

EPHESIANS 1:7-8

331

CROSSWORD

ACROSS

1. "BUT WHEN THE KINDNESS AND LOVE OF GOD OUR SAVIOR _____."
2. "HE _____ US."
3. "NOT BECAUSE OF _____ THINGS WE HAD DONE."
4. "BUT BECAUSE OF HIS _____."

DOWN

1. "HE SAVED US THROUGH THE _____."
2. "OF REBIRTH AND _____ BY THE HOLY SPIRIT."
3. "WHOM HE POURED OUT ON US _____."
4. "THROUGH JESUS _____ OUR SAVIOR."

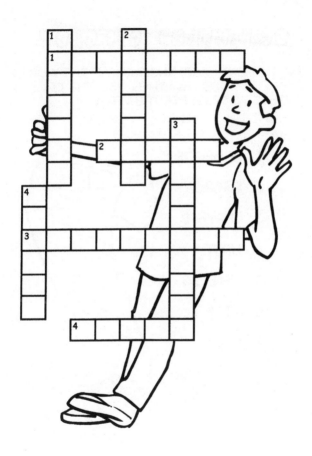

SCRAMBLED CIRCLES

ON THE NEXT PAGE, UNSCRAMBLE THE WORDS
IN THE LIST BELOW. THEN USE THE CIRCLED
LETTERS TO COMPLETE THE VERSE.

1. RFDEEOF

2. EADRGR

3. LERYFIB

4. URTE

5. NHTISG

6. TIGF

7. LULF

8. ARETNLE

1. _ _ ◯ _ _ _ _
2. _ _ _ ◯ _ _
3. _ _ ◯ _ _ _ _
4. ◯ _ _ _
5. _ ◯ _ _ _ _
6. _ _ ◯ _
7. _ ◯ _ _
8. _ _ _ _ _ _ ◯

"WITH THE HELP OF SILAS, WHOM I REGARD AS A _ _ _ _ _ _ _ _ BROTHER, I HAVE WRITTEN TO YOU BRIEFLY, ENCOURAGING YOU."

1 PETER 5:12

ASK YOURSELF

WHAT HAVE YOU LEARNED SO FAR? FIND OUT
BY ANSWERING THE QUESTIONS BELOW.

1. WHAT DO WE HAVE WITH GOD?

ROMANS 5:1–2

_____

2. WHAT DO WE NOW STAND IN?

ROMANS 5:1–2

_____

3. HOW DOES PAUL DESCRIBE THIS
   GRACE THAT SAVES US?

EPHESIANS 2:8–9

_____

4. CAN WE WORK TO EARN GOD'S GRACE?

_____

5. WHAT DID GOD DO FOR US?

EPHESIANS 2:4–5

_____

6. WHY DID GOD MAKE US ALIVE WITH CHRIST?

EPHESIANS 2:4–5

_____

▰ANSWER PAGES▰

PG. 9

1. GOSPEL   PROPHETS

2. POWER   SPIRIT

3. GRACE   FATHER

    CHRIST

PG. 11

"I AM NOT A S H A M E D OF THE G O S P E L. BECAUSE IT IS THE P O W E R OF G O D FOR THE S A L V A T I O N OF E V E R Y O N E WHO BELIEVES: FIRST FOR THE J E W, THEN FOR THE G E N T I L E."

ROMANS 1:16

PG. 13

"T H E W R A T H O F G O D I S B E I N G R E V E A L E D F R O M H E A V E N A G A I N S T A L L T H E G O D L E S S- N E S S A N D W I C K E D- N E S S O F M E N W H O S U P P R E S S T H E T R U T H B Y T H E I R W I C K E D- N E S S. S I N C E W H A T M A Y B E K N O W N A B O U T G O D I S P L A I N T O T H E M. B E C A U S E G O D H A S M A D E I T P L A I N T O T H E M."

ROMANS 1:18-19

339

PG. 15

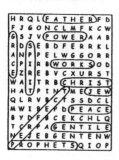

PG. 17

For ever since the <u>world</u> was <u>created</u>, people have seen the <u>earth</u> and sky. Through everything <u>God</u> made, they can <u>clearly</u> see his <u>invisible</u> qualities—his eternal <u>power</u> and divine <u>nature</u>. So they have no <u>excuse</u> for not <u>knowing</u> God.

ROMANS 1:20, NLT

PG. 19

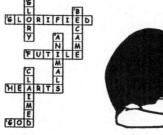

"YOU, THEREFORE, HAVE NO EXCUSE, YOU WHO PASS JUDGMENT ON SOMEONE ELSE. FOR AT WHATEVER POINT YOU JUDGE THE OTHER, YOU ARE CONDEMNING YOURSELF, BECAUSE YOU WHO PASS JUDGMENT DO THE SAME THINGS."

ROMANS 2:1

Do you <u>suppose</u>, O man—you who <u>judge</u> those who <u>practice</u> such things and yet do them <u>yourself</u>—that you will <u>escape</u> the <u>judgment</u> of God? Or do you <u>presume</u> on the <u>riches</u> of his <u>kindness</u> and forbearance and patience, not <u>knowing</u> that <u>God's</u> kindness is <u>meant</u> to lead you to <u>repentance</u>?

ROMANS 2:3-4, ESV

"NOW Y O U, IF YOU CALL Y O U R S E L F A JEW; IF YOU R E L Y ON THE LAW AND B R A G ABOUT YOUR R E L A T I O N S H I P TO G O D; IF YOU KNOW HIS W I L L AND A P P R O V E OF WHAT IS S U P E R I O R BECAUSE YOU ARE I N S T R U C T E D BY THE LAW."

ROMANS 2:17-18

1. CONVINCED   BLIND
   LIGHT
2. INSTRUCTOR   FOOLISH
3. LAW   TRUTH
3. TEACH

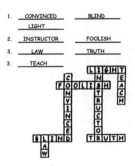

341

"THERE IS NO
ONE RIGHTEOUS,
NOT EVEN ONE;
THERE IS NO
ONE WHO UNDER-
STANDS, NO ONE
WHO SEEKS GOD.
ALL HAVE TURNED
AWAY, THEY HAVE
TOGETHER BECOME
WORTHLESS; THERE
IS NO ONE WHO
DOES GOOD, NOT
EVEN ONE."

ROMANS 3:10-12

1. ___TURNED___   ___WORTHLESS___

2. ___ONE___   ___GOOD___

3. ___THROATS___   ___DECEIT___

___VIPERS___   ___LIPS___

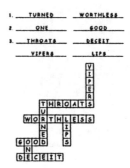

"THEIR M O U T H S ARE
FULL OF C U R S I N G
AND BITTERNESS. THEIR FEET
ARE S W I F T TO SHED
B L O O D; RUIN AND
M I S E R Y MARK THEIR
WAYS, AND THE WAY OF
P E A C E THEY DO NOT
KNOW."

ROMANS 3:14-17

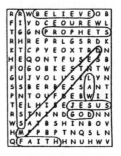

ABCDEFGHIJKLMNOPQRST
UVWXYZ

"FOR ALL HAVE
SINNED AND FALL
SHORT OF THE
GLORY OF GOD,
AND ARE JUST-
IFIED FREELY
BY HIS GRACE
THROUGH THE
REDEMPTION THAT
CAME BY CHRIST
JESUS."

ROMANS 3:23–24

PG. 43

"WHERE IS _BOASTING_ THEN? IT IS
EXCLUDED. BY WHAT _LAW_? OF
WORKS? NAY: BUT BY THE LAW OF
FAITH. THEREFORE WE CONCLUDE
THAT A _MAN_ IS _JUSTIFIED_
BY FAITH WITHOUT THE _DEEDS_ OF
THE LAW. IS HE THE _GOD_ OF THE
JEWS ONLY? IS HE NOT ALSO OF
THE GENTILES? YES, OF THE
GENTILES ALSO."

ROMANS 3:27–29, KJV

"THEREFORE, SINCE WE HAVE BEEN J U S T I F I E D THROUGH F A I T H , WE HAVE P E A C E WITH GOD THROUGH OUR L O R D JESUS CHRIST, THROUGH WHOM WE HAVE GAINED ACCESS BY FAITH INTO THIS G R A C E IN WHICH WE NOW S T A N D ."

ROMANS 5:1-2

"N O T O N L Y S O, B U T W E A L S O R E J O I C E I N O U R S U F F E R I N G S, B E C A U S E W E K N O W T H A T S U F F E R I N G P R O D U C E S P E R S E V E R A N C E; P E R S E V E R A N C E, C H A R A C T E R; A N D C H A R A C T E R, H O P E."

ROMANS 5:3-4

"For when we were yet without strength, in due time Christ died for the ungodly. For scarcely for a righteous man will one die: yet peradventure for a good man some would even dare to die."

ROMANS 5:6-7, KJV

ABCDEFGHIJKLMNOPQRST
UVWXYZ

"BUT GOD DEMON-
STRATES HIS OWN
LOVE FOR US IN
THIS: WHILE WE
WERE   STILL
SINNERS, CHRIST
DIED FOR US."

ROMANS 5:8

"And since we have been <u>made</u> right in God's <u>sight</u> by the blood of <u>Christ</u>, he will certainly <u>save</u> us from God's <u>condemnation</u>. For since our <u>friendship</u> with God was restored by the <u>death</u> of his Son while we were still his <u>enemies</u>, we will certainly be saved through the <u>life</u> of his <u>Son</u>."

ROMANS 5:9-10, NLT

"THEREFORE, JUST AS S I N
ENTERED THE W O R L D
THROUGH ONE M A N, AND
D E A T H THROUGH S I N,
AND IN THIS WAY DEATH CAME TO
A L L MEN, BECAUSE ALL
S I N N E D —FOR BEFORE THE
L A W WAS GIVEN, SIN WAS IN
THE W O R L D."

ROMANS 5:12-13

1. TRESPASS   DIED
2. GOD'S   GRACE
    CAME
3. CHRIST   OVERFLOW

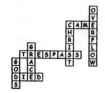

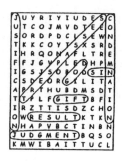

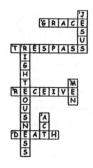

"FOR JUST AS THROUGH THE
D I S O B E D I E N C E
OF THE ONE MAN THE MANY WERE
MADE S I N N E R S, SO
ALSO THROUGH THE
O B E D I E N C E
OF THE ONE M A N THE
M A N Y WILL BE MADE
R I G H T E O U S."

ROMANS 5:19

346

"WHAT SHALL WE SAY, THEN? SHALL WE GO ON SINNING SO THAT GRACE MAY INCREASE? BY NO MEANS! WE DIED TO SIN; HOW CAN WE LIVE IN IT ANY LONGER?"

ROMANS 6:1-2

"Do you not <u>know</u> that all of us who have been <u>baptized</u> into Christ <u>Jesus</u> were baptized into his death? We were <u>buried</u> therefore with him by baptism into death, in <u>order</u> that, just as Christ was <u>raised</u> from the dead by the <u>glory</u> of the Father, we too might <u>walk</u> in newness of <u>life</u>."

ROMANS 6:3-4, ESV

1. ___UNITED___ ___DEATH___
   ___HIM___
2. ___CRUCIFIED___ ___MIGHT___
3. ___DIED___ ___FREED___

"When he <u>died</u>, he died <u>once</u> to <u>break</u> the <u>power</u> of sin. But now that he <u>lives</u>, he lives for the glory of <u>God</u>. So you also should <u>consider</u> yourselves to be dead to the power of <u>sin</u> and <u>alive</u> to God through <u>Christ</u> Jesus."

ROMANS 6:10-11, NLT

ABCDEFGHIJKLMNOPQRST
UVWXYZ

"FOR SIN SHALL
NOT BE YOUR
MASTER, BECAUSE
YOU ARE NOT
UNDER LAW, BUT
UNDER GRACE."

ROMANS 6:14

"SO, MY BROTHERS,
YOU ALSO DIED TO
THE LAW THROUGH
THE BODY OF
CHRIST, THAT YOU
MIGHT BELONG TO
ANOTHER, TO HIM
WHO WAS RAISED
FROM THE DEAD,
IN ORDER THAT
WE MIGHT BEAR
FRUIT TO GOD."

ROMANS 7:4

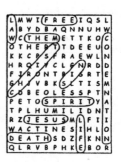

A B C D E F G H I J K L M N O P Q R S T
U V W X Y Z

"FOR WHAT THE LAW WAS POWER-
LESS TO DO IN THAT IT WAS
WEAKENED BY THE SINFUL
NATURE. GOD DID BY SENDING
HIS OWN SON IN THE LIKENESS
OF SINFUL MAN TO BE A SIN
OFFERING."

ROMANS 8:3

"For what the <u>law</u> could not do, in that it was <u>weak</u> through the flesh, <u>God</u> sending his own <u>Son</u> in the likeness of sinful <u>flesh</u>, and for sin, <u>condemned</u> sin in the flesh: That the <u>righteousness</u> of the law <u>might</u> be fulfilled in us, who <u>walk</u> not after the flesh, but after the <u>Spirit</u>."

ROMANS 8:3-4, KJV

"THOSE WHO LIVE ACCORDING TO THE SINFUL NATURE HAVE THEIR MINDS SET ON WHAT THAT NATURE DESIRES; BUT THOSE WHO LIVE IN ACCORDANCE WITH THE SPIRIT HAVE THEIR MINDS SET ON WHAT THE SPIRIT DESIRES."

ROMANS 8:5

PG. 95

"YOU, HOWEVER,
ARE CONTROLLED
NOT BY THE
SINFUL NATURE
BUT BY THE
SPIRIT. IF THE
SPIRIT OF GOD
LIVES IN YOU."

ROMANS 8:9

PG. 97

1. CHRIST   DEAD
    SPIRIT   ALIVE
2. RAISED   LIFE
    MORTAL   BODIES

PG. 99

"FOR YOU DID NOT
R E C E I V E A
S P I R I T THAT MAKES
YOU A S L A V E AGAIN TO
F E A R, BUT YOU RECEIVED
THE S P I R I T OF
S O N S H I P. AND BY
HIM WE C R Y, 'A B B A,
FATHER.'"

ROMANS 8:15

PG. 101

PG. 103

"WE KNOW THAT THE WHOLE CREATION HAS BEEN GROANING AS IN THE PAINS OF CHILDBIRTH RIGHT UP TO THE PRESENT TIME."

ROMANS 8:22

PG. 105

ABCDEFGHIJKLMNOPQRST
UVWXYZ

"NOT ONLY SO BUT WE OUR-SELVES, WHO HAVE THE FIRST-FRUITS OF THE SPIRIT GROAN INWARDLY AS WE WAIT EAGERLY FOR OUR ADOP-TION AS SONS, THE REDEMP-TION OF OUR BODIES."

ROMANS 8:23

PG. 107

"For we are <u>saved</u> by hope: but <u>hope</u> that is <u>seen</u> is not hope: for <u>what</u> a <u>man</u> seeth, <u>why</u> doth he yet hope for? But if we hope for that we see <u>not</u>, then do we with <u>patience</u> wait for it."

ROMANS 8:24–25, KJV

PG. 109

1. WEAKNESS
2. PRAY   HIMSELF
   GROANS   WORDS
3. SEARCHES   SPIRIT
   INTERCEDES

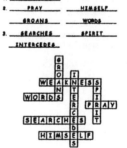

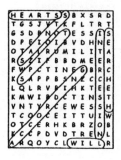

"AND WE KNOW THAT IN ALL THINGS GOD WORKS FOR THE GOOD OF THOSE WHO LOVE HIM, WHO HAVE BEEN CALLED ACCORDING TO HIS PURPOSE."

ROMANS 8:28

"For whom he did <u>foreknow</u>, he also did <u>predestinate</u> to be <u>conformed</u> to the <u>image</u> of his <u>Son</u>, that he <u>might</u> be the <u>firstborn</u> among many <u>brethren</u>."

ROMANS 8:29, KJV

1. PREDESTINED   JUSTIFIED

    GLORIFIED

2.   SHALL   THIS

3.   GOD   AGAINST

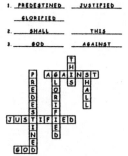

PG. 119

"HE WHO DID <u>N</u><u>O</u><u>T</u>

<u>S</u><u>P</u><u>A</u><u>R</u><u>E</u> HIS OWN

<u>S</u><u>O</u><u>N</u>, BUT GAVE <u>H</u><u>I</u><u>M</u>

UP FOR US <u>A</u><u>L</u><u>L</u>—HOW

WILL HE NOT <u>A</u><u>L</u><u>S</u><u>O</u>,

ALONG WITH <u>H</u><u>I</u><u>M</u>,

<u>G</u><u>R</u><u>A</u><u>C</u><u>I</u><u>O</u><u>U</u><u>S</u><u>L</u><u>Y</u>

GIVE US ALL <u>T</u><u>H</u><u>I</u><u>N</u><u>G</u><u>S</u>?"

ROMANS 8:32

PG. 121

"For I am <u>persuaded</u>, that neither <u>death</u>, nor life, nor <u>angels</u>,
nor principalities, nor <u>powers</u>,
nor things <u>present</u>, nor things to
<u>come</u>, Nor height, nor <u>depth</u>, nor
any other <u>creature</u>, shall be able
to <u>separate</u> us from the <u>love</u> of
God, which is in Christ <u>Jesus</u> our
<u>Lord</u>."

ROMANS 8:38-39, KJV

PG. 123

A B C D E F G H I J K L M N O P Q R S T
U V W X Y Z

<u>WHAT THEN SHALL
WE SAY? THAT THE
GENTILES, WHO
DID NOT PURSUE
RIGHTEOUSNESS,
HAVE OBTAINED
IT, A RIGHTEOUS-
NESS THAT IS BY
FAITH.</u>"

ROMANS 9:30

PG. 125

353

"BROTHERS, MY HEART'S DESIRE AND PRAYER TO GOD FOR THE ISRAELITES IS THAT THEY MAY BE SAVED."

ROMANS 10:1

"FOR I CAN TESTIFY ABOUT THEM THAT THEY ARE ZEALOUS FOR GOD, BUT THEIR ZEAL IS NOT BASED ON KNOWLEDGE."

ROMANS 10:2

PG. 131

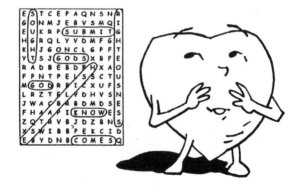

1. RIGHTEOUSNESS   EVERYONE
   BELIEVETH
2. WORD   HEART
3. CONFESS   MOUTH
   RAISED

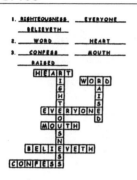

ABCDEFGHIJKLMNOPQRST
UVWXYZ

"FOR IT IS WITH
YOUR HEART THAT
YOU BELIEVE AND
ARE JUSTIFIED,
AND IT IS WITH
YOUR MOUTH THAT
YOU CONFESS
AND ARE SAVED."

ROMANS 10:10

For the <u>Scripture</u> says, "Everyone who <u>believes</u> in him will not be put to <u>shame</u>." For there is no <u>distinction</u> between <u>Jew</u> and Greek; for the <u>same</u> Lord is Lord of <u>all</u>, bestowing his <u>riches</u> on all who <u>call</u> on him. For "<u>everyone</u> who calls on the <u>name</u> of the Lord will be <u>saved</u>."

ROMANS 10:11-13, ESV

"I ASK THEN:
DID GOD REJECT
HIS PEOPLE?
BY NO MEANS!
I AM AN ISRAEL-
ITE MYSELF,
A DESCENDANT
OF ABRAHAM,
FROM THE TRIBE
OF BENJAMIN."

ROMANS 11:1

PG. 143

"**G O D** DID NOT **R E J E C T**

HIS **P E O P L E**, WHOM HE

F O R E K N E W. DON'T YOU KNOW

WHAT THE **S C R I P T U R E**

SAYS IN THE **P A S S A G E**

ABOUT **E L I J A H** – HOW HE

A P P E A L E D TO **G O D**

AGAINST ISRAEL."

ROMANS 11:2

PG. 145

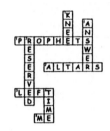

PG. 147

PG. 149

"**T H E R E F O R E,**
I U R G E Y O U,
B R O T H E R S, I N
V I E W O F G O D'S
M E R C Y, T O O F F E R
Y O U R B O D I E S
A S L I V I N G S A C R I -
F I C E S, H O L Y A N D
P L E A S I N G T O G O D
– T H I S I S Y O U R
S P I R I T U A L A C T
O F W O R S H I P."

ROMANS 12:1

"And be not <u>conformed</u> to this <u>world</u>: but be ye <u>transformed</u> by the <u>renewing</u> of your <u>mind</u>, that ye may <u>prove</u> what is that <u>good</u>, and <u>acceptable</u>, and perfect, <u>will</u> of <u>God</u>."

ROMANS 12:2, KJV

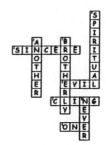

A B C D E F G H I J K L M N O P Q R S T
U V W X Y Z

"BLESS THOSE WHO

PERSECUTE YOU;

BLESS AND DO NOT

CURSE. REJOICE

WITH THOSE WHO

REJOICE; MOURN

WITH THOSE WHO

MOURN."

ROMANS 12:14-15

"ON THE C O N T R A R Y:

IF YOUR E N E M Y IS

H U N G R Y, F E E D

HIM; IF HE IS T H I R S T Y,

GIVE H I M SOMETHING TO

D R I N K. IN D O I N G

THIS, YOU W I L L H E A P

B U R N I N G C O A L S

ON HIS H E A D."

ROMANS 12:20

PG. 159

EVERYONE   SUBMIT
HIMSELF   GOVERNING
EXCEPT   ESTABLISHED
AUTHORITIES   BEEN
GOD

PG. 163

PG. 165

"ACCEPT H I M WHOSE
F A I T H IS W E A K
WITHOUT P A S S I N G
J U D G M E N T
ON D I S P U T A B L E
MATTERS."

ROMANS 14:1

"We who are <u>strong</u> must be <u>considerate</u> of those who are <u>sensitive</u> about <u>things</u> like this. We <u>must</u> not just <u>please</u> ourselves. We should <u>help</u> others do what is <u>right</u> and <u>build</u> them up in the <u>Lord</u>."

ROMANS 15:1-2, NLT

A B C D E F G H I J K L M N O P Q R S T
U V W X Y Z

"FOR EVEN CHRIST
DID NOT PLEASE
HIMSELF BUT,
AS IT IS WRITTEN:
THE INSULTS OF
THOSE WHO INSULT
YOU HAVE FALLEN
ON ME."

ROMANS 15:3

"Now the _God_ of hope <u>fill</u> you with all <u>joy</u> and peace in <u>believing</u>, that <u>ye</u> may <u>abound</u> in <u>hope</u>, <u>through</u> the <u>power</u> of the Holy <u>Ghost</u>."

ROMANS 15:13, KJV

359

```
H O F R L C I M T
D B T J G N Q A K
I P M V O H D P F
C R A K T E R V B
L S W H W V W G Q
Q P N W L B O C I
F G V D T R A N U
K A I Q M O H P L
M C N S G B K D F
```

"For the law was given by Moses, but grace and truth came by J e s u s Christ."

JOHN 1:17, KJV

"So why are you now challenging God by burdening the Gentile believers with a yoke that neither we nor our ancestors were able to bear? We believe that we are all saved the same way, by the undeserved grace of the Lord Jesus."

ACTS 15:10-11, NLT

1. C A M E
2. M O S E S
3. G I V E N
4. T R Y
5. C H R I S T
6. N E C K S
7. Y O U
8. J E S U S

"SO THEN, JUST AS YOU RECEIVED CHRIST AS LORD, C O N T I N U E TO LIVE IN HIM."

COLOSSIANS 2:6

1. MINISTRY   ENGRAVED

    GLORY   STEADILY

2. CONDEMNS   MORE

3. FOR   COMPARISON

"NOW THE <u>L O R D</u> IS THE
       25 31 34 14

<u>S P I R I T</u>, AND WHERE THE
35 32 22 34 22 36

SPIRIT OF THE LORD IS, THERE IS

<u>F R E E D O M</u>. AND WE, WHO
16 34 15 15 14 31 26

WITH UNVEILED <u>F A C E S</u> ALL
             16 11 13 15 35

<u>R E F L E C T</u> THE LORD'S
34 15 16 25 15 13 36

<u>G L O R Y</u>,   ARE   BEING
17 25 31 34 44

TRANSFORMED   INTO   HIS

<u>L I K E N E S S</u> WITH EVER-
25 22 24 15 27 15 35 35

INCREASING   GLORY,   WHICH

<u>C O M E S</u>   FROM   THE
13 31 26 15 35

<u>L O R D</u> WHO IS THE SPIRIT."
25 31 34 14

2 CORINTHIANS 3:17-18

```
D  J  E  M  B  Q  L  P  E
N  C  U  I  O  K  G (W) S
K  S  P  V  X  D  S  N  V
O (R) F  L  M  V  F  C  J
F  G  Q  X  D  U  I  B  P
J  L (A) K  V  O  Q  M  C
N  U  M  C  S  X  L (T) G
B  E  O  I  U  K  Q  I  N
P  G  X  D (H) F  E  J  B
```

"For which things' sake the <u>wrath</u> of God cometh on the children of disobedience."

COLOSSIANS 3:6, KJV

ASK YOURSELF
ANSWERS

1. THE LAW.

2. GRACE AND TRUTH.

3. A NEW COVENANT.

4. THE SPIRIT.

5. THE LETTER KILLS.

6. THE SPIRIT GIVES LIFE.

"You <u>yourselves</u> have seen what I did to the <u>Egyptians</u>, and how I <u>bore</u> you on eagles' <u>wings</u> and brought you to <u>myself</u>. Now <u>therefore</u>, if you will indeed <u>obey</u> my <u>voice</u> and keep my <u>covenant</u>, you shall be my treasured possession among all <u>peoples</u>, for all the earth is mine."

EXODUS 19:4–5, ESV

G	M	J	Q	H	O	D	I	P
R	C	F	W	K	Z	U	W	R
K	T	N	Z	P	B	J	Q	M
D	I	U	S	T	R	F	Z	W
O	B	H	C	Z	G	N	C	D
P	G	J	Q	F	W	J	L	O
T	N	F	U	P	H	A	U	T
V	C	O	R	M	N	G	I	B
K	I	E	H	D	B	M	K	Q

"WE KNOW THAT THE LAW IS SPIRITUAL; BUT I AM UNSPIRITUAL, SOLD AS A S L A V E TO SIN."

ROMANS 7:14

1. S O L D
2. D A R E
3. C H R I S T
4. L A W
5. C O V E N A N T
6. R A R E L Y
7. E A G L E
8. D I E D

"Theefore no one will be UNDERLINED righteous in his sight by observing the law; rather, through the law we become conscious of sin."

DECLARED

ROMANS 3:20

"IF YOU F U L L Y OBEY THE
           16 37 25 44

LORD YOUR G O D AND CAREFULLY
           17 31 14

F O L L O W   ALL   HIS
16 31 25 25 31 42

C O M M A N D S I GIVE YOU
13 31 26 26 11 27 14 35

TODAY, THE L O R D YOUR GOD
            25 31 34 14

WILL SET YOU H I G H ABOVE
              21 22 17 21

ALL THE N A T I O N S ON
        27 11 36 22 31 27 35

EARTH."

DEUTERONOMY 28:1

"   HOWEVER   ,   IF   YOU

DO   NOT   OBEY   THE

LORD   YOUR   GOD   AND

DO   NOT   CAREFULLY

FOLLOW   ALL   HIS

COMMANDS   AND

DECREES   I   AM

GIVING   YOU   TODAY

ALL   THESE   CURSES

WILL   COME   UPON   YOU

AND   OVERTAKE   YOU "

DEUTERONOMY 28:15

A B C D E F G H I J K L M N O P Q R S T
U V W X Y Z

" WHAT ,   THEN   ,   WAS
THE   PURPOSE   OF
THE   LAW ?   IT   WAS
ADDED   BECAUSE   OF
   TRANSGRESSIONS
UNTIL   THE   SEED
TO   WHOM   THE
PROMISE   REFERRED
HAD   COME   THE   LAW
WAS   PUT   INTO
EFFECT   THROUGH
ANGELS   BY   A
MEDIATOR ."

GALATIANS 3:19

363

1. HOLY   COMMANDMENT

   RIGHTEOUS   GOOD

2. SPIRITUAL   UNSPIRITUAL

   SLAVE   SIN

	G		U								
C	O	M	M	A	N	D	M	E	N	T	
	O		S								H
	D		P								O
		S	I	R	I	T	U	A	L		L
			R								Y
	R	I	I	G	H	T	E	O	U	S	
			U							I	
			A							N	
		S	L	A	V	E					

ASK YOURSELF
ANSWERS

1. EVERYTHING THE LORD HAD SAID.

2. UNTIL THE SEED CAME.

3. JESUS CHRIST.

4. HOLY, RIGHTEOUS AND GOOD.

5. IT IS SPIRITUAL.

6. YES!

```
O  C  N  I  V  K  X  H  R
H  J  W  G  B  P  F  J  V
F  M  A  L  O  ■ (S) N  L
R  V  I  X  C  K  T  G  B
(E) O  G  T  J  M  C  W  P
P  K  B  W (E) L  I  A  O
A  T  L  C  R  G  X  M  H
X  I (D) H  M  W  F  J  N
N  R  P  F  V  A  K  T  B
```

"Wherefore then serveth the law?
It was added because of transgressions, till the s e e d should
come to whom the promise was
made; and it was ordained by angels in the hand of a mediator."

GALATIANS 3:19, KJV

364

A B C D E F G H I J K L M N O P Q R S T
U V W X Y Z

" __THE__ __PROMISES__
__WERE__ __SPOKEN__ __TO__
__ABRAHAM__ __AND__ __TO__
__HIS__ __SEED__ . __THE__
__SCRIPTURE__ __DOES__
__NOT__ __SAY__ ' __AND__ __TO__
__SEEDS__ ,' __MEANING__
__MANY__ __PEOPLE__ , __BUT__
' __AND__ __TO__ __YOUR__
__SEED__ ,' __MEANING__
__ONE__ __PERSON__ __WHO__
__IS__ __CHRIST__ . "

GALATIANS 3:16

ADDED   TRESPASS
INCREASE   RIGHTEOUSNESS
ETERNAL   CHRIST

E T E R N A L
R
I
C   G
H   T   H
R   T   T
I N C R E A S E
S   E   D   O
T   S   D   U
S   E   S
P   D   N
A   E
S   S
S

"But we <u>know</u> that the law is <u>good</u>, if a man use it <u>lawfully</u>; Knowing this, that the law is not made for a <u>righteous</u> man, but for the lawless and <u>disobedient</u>, for the ungodly and for <u>sinners</u>, for unholy and profane, for <u>murderers</u> of fathers and murderers of <u>mothers</u>, for manslayers, For whoremongers, for them that <u>defile</u> themselves with mankind, for mensteelers, for <u>liars</u>, for perjured persons, and if there be any other thing that is <u>contrary</u> to sound <u>doctrine</u>."

1 TIMOTHY 1:8-10, KJV

" T H E R E F O R E NO ONE
  36 21 15 34 15 16 31 34 15

WILL BE D E C L A R E D
             14 15 13 28 11 34 15 14

R I G H T E O U S IN HIS
34 22 17 21 36 15 31 37 35

SIGHT BY O B S E R V I N G
         31 12 35 15 34 41 22 27 17

THE   LAW;   R A T H E R ,
             34 11 36 21 15 34

THROUGH THE L A W WE BECOME
            25 11 42

C O N S C I O U S   OF
13 31 27 35 13 22 31 37 35

S I N . "
35 22 27

ROMANS 3:20

PG. 221

" ___ THEREFORE ___ , ___ JUST
AS ___ SIN ___ ENTERED
THE ___ WORLD ___ THROUGH
ONE ___ MAN ___ AND ___ DEATH
THROUGH ___ SIN ___ AND without
IN ___ THIS ___ WAY
DEATH ___ CAME ___ TO
ALL ___ MEN , ___ BECAUSE
ALL ___ SINNED ___ — FOR
BEFORE ___ THE ___ LAW
WAS ___ GIVEN , ___ SIN
WAS ___ IN ___ THE
WORLD ."

ROMANS 5:12–13

PG. 223

1. ___ THEN ___ CERTAINLY
___ HAVE ___ COVETING
2. ___ SEIZING ___ COVETOUS
___ DESIRE ___ SIN

PG. 225

"For I was <u>alive</u> without the law
once: but <u>when</u> the <u>commandment</u>
came, <u>sin</u> revived, and I <u>died</u>. And
the commandment, which was
<u>ordained</u> to <u>life</u>, I <u>found</u> to be
unto <u>death</u>."

ROMANS 7:9-10, KJV

PG. 227

A B C D E F G H I J K L M N O P Q R S T
U V W X Y Z

" ___ FOR ___ SIN ___ SEIZING
___ THE ___ OPPORTUNITY
___ AFFORDED ___ BY ___ THE
___ COMMANDMENT ,
___ DECEIVED ___ ME ___ AND
___ THROUGH ___ THE
___ COMMANDMENT ___ PUT
ME ___ TO ___ DEATH . ___ SO
THEN , ___ THE ___ LAW ___ IS
___ HOLY , ___ AND ___ THE
___ COMMANDMENT ___ IS
HOLY , ___ RIGHTEOUS
AND ___ GOOD ."

ROMANS 7:11–12

366

1. R O **B** E
2. U T T **E** R L Y
3. D E **C** E I V E
4. G **O** O D
5. **M** E A N S
6. L I F **E**

"DID THAT WHICH IS GOOD, THEN,
B E C O M E DEATH TO ME?
BY NO MEANS."

ROMANS 7:13

PG. 232–233

ASK YOURSELF
ANSWERS

1. IT IS A PRISONER OF SIN.

2. THROUGH FAITH IN JESUS CHRIST.

3. THOSE WHO BELIEVE.

4. THE LAW.

5. UNTIL FAITH SHOULD BE REVEALED.

6. SO THAT WE MIGHT BE JUSTIFIED
   BY FAITH.

1. FORMER   REGULATION
    ASIDE
2. LAW   PERFECT
    BETTER   INTRODUCED
    DRAW

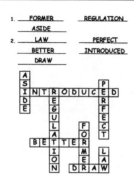

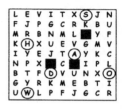

"The old system under the law of
Moses was only a s h a d o w, a dim
preview of the good things to come,
not the good things themselves."

HEBREWS 10:1, NLT

"FOR   WHAT   THE   LAW   WAS

P O W E R L E S S TO DO IN
32 31 42 15 34 25 15 35 35

THAT IT WAS W E A K E N E D
42 15 11 24 15 27 15 14

BY THE SINFUL N A T U R E
27 11 36 37 34 15

G O D DID BY SENDING HIS OWN
17 31 14

S O N IN THE LIKENESS OF
35 31 27

S I N F U L MAN TO BE A SIN
35 22 27 16 37 25

O F F E R I N G. AND SO HE
31 16 16 15 34 22 27 17

CONDEMNED S I N IN SINFUL
35 22 27

MAN."

ROMANS 8:30

" IS   THE   LAW ,
    THEREFORE   OPPOSED
TO   THE   PROMISES
OF   GOD ?   ABSOLUTELY
NOT !   FOR   IF   A   LAW
HAD   BEEN   GIVEN
THAT   COULD   IMPART
LIFE   THEN   RIGHTEOUS -
NESS   WOULD   CERTAINLY
HAVE   COME   BY   THE
LAW ."

GALATIANS 3:21

PG. 245

1. J U S T I (F) I E D

2. L (A) W

3. W (I) L L

4. C H R I S (T)

5. T (H) R O U G H

"KNOW THAT A MAN IS NOT JUSTIFIED BY OBSERVING THE LAW, BUT BY F A I T H IN JESUS CHRIST."
GALATIANS 2:16

PG. 247

A B C D E F G H I J K L M N O P Q R S T
U V W X Y Z

" BUT BECAUSE OF HIS GREAT LOVE FOR US, GOD, WHO IS RICH IN MERCY MADE US ALIVE WITH CHRIST EVEN WHEN WE WERE DEAD IN TRANSGRESSIONS — IT IS BY GRACE YOU HAVE BEEN SAVED ."

EPHESIANS 2:4—5

PG. 248—249

ASK YOURSELF
ANSWERS

1. IT IS SET ASIDE.

2. NO. . . NOT EVER.

3. BY FAITH IN JESUS CHRIST.

4. NO.

5. THE LAW BRINGS DEATH.

6. GOD.

THINK
D I N K
THINK
S
ABOLISH
UPPET
NPPATHEM
THEMTTE
ILAR

" HE SAID TO THEM ,
' THIS IS WHAT I
TOLD YOU WHILE I
WAS STILL WITH
YOU : EVERYTHING
MUST BE FULFILLED
THAT IS WRITTEN
ABOUT ME IN THE
LAW OF MOSES ,
THE PROPHETS AND
THE PSALMS .' "

LUKE 24:44

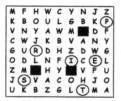

"For we do not have a high p r i e s t
who is unable to sympathize with
our weaknesses."

HEBREWS 4:15, ESV

"FOR THE W A G E S OF S I N
42 11 17 18 35   35 22 27
IS D E A T H . BUT THE
14 15 11 36 21
G I F T OF G O D IS
17 22 16 36   17 31 14
E T E R N A L L I F E
15 36 15 34 27 11 29   25 22 16 15
IN CHRIST J E S U S OUR
23 15 35 37 35
L O R D ."
25 31 34 14

ROMANS 6:23

1. E T E R N (A) L
2. G I F (T)
3. W I T H (O) U T
4. U (N) A B L E
5. P R (I) E S T
6. S I (N)
7. W A (G) E S

"HE IS THE A T O N I N G
SACRIFICE FOR OUR SINS, AND NOT
ONLY FOR OURS BUT ALSO FOR THE SINS
OF THE WHOLE WORLD."

1 JOHN 2:2

"You were <u>dead</u> because of your sins and because your <u>sinful</u> nature was not yet <u>cut</u> away. Then <u>God</u> made you <u>alive</u> with Christ, for he <u>forgave</u> all our sins. He <u>canceled</u> the record of the <u>charges</u> against us and took it away by <u>nailing</u> it to the <u>cross</u>."

COLOSSIANS 2:13-14, NLT

1. POWERLESS   WEAKENED
   SENDING   SINFUL
2. CONDEMNED   DO
   LIVE   SPIRIT

ASK YOURSELF
ANSWERS

1. TO FUFILL IT.

2. HE WOULD.

3. HE CANCELLED IT.

4. HE NAILED IT TO THE CROSS.

5. ON THE CROSS.

6. NO!

PG. 271

"<u>Christ</u> hath <u>redeemed</u> us from the curse of the <u>law</u>, being <u>made</u> a <u>curse</u> for us: for it is <u>written</u>, <u>Cursed</u> is every <u>one</u> that <u>hangeth</u> on a <u>tree</u>."

GALATIANS 3:13, KJV

PG. 273

"FOR YOU <u>K N O W</u> THAT
                24 27 31 42
IT WAS NOT WITH
<u>P E R I S H A B L E</u>
32 15 34 22 35 21 11 12 25 15
THINGS SUCH AS <u>S I L V E R</u>
                     35 22 25 41 15 34
OR <u>G O L D</u> THAT YOU WERE
   17 31 25 14
REDEEMED FROM THE <u>E M P T Y</u>
                   15 26 32 36 44
WAY OF <u>L I F E</u> HANDED DOWN
       25 22 16 15
TO YOU FROM YOUR
<u>F O R E F A T H E R S</u>,
16 31 34 15 16 11 36 21 15 34 35
BUT WITH THE <u>P R E C I O U S</u>
             32 34 15 13 22 31 37 35
BLOOD OF CHRIST, A <u>L A M B</u>
                  25 11 26 12
WITHOUT BLEMISH OR
<u>D E F E C T</u>."
14 15 16 15 13 36

1 PETER 1:18–19

PG. 275

1.   TRUTH   FREE
2. DESCENDANTS   ANYONE
3.   REPLIED   EVERYONE

```
          R E P L I E D
        D         V
  F R E E         E
        S         R
        C         Y
        E         O
  A N Y O N E     N
        D         E
        A
        N
      T R U T H
        S
```

372

PG. 277

" BUT   THE   SCRIPTURE
DECLARES   THAT   THE
WHOLE   WORLD   IS   A
PRISONER   OF   SIN
SO   THAT   WHAT   WAS
PROMISED   ,   BEING
GIVEN   THROUGH
FAITH   IN   JESUS
CHRIST   ,   MIGHT   BE
GIVEN   TO   THOSE
WHO   BELIEVE   ."

GALATIANS 3:22

PG. 279

Crossword:

```
M E A N S
O   E
R  N T E R E D
 E        E
 R      H A V I N G
 N      T
 A  G   H
B L O O D
    D
```

PG. 281

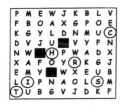

"There is therefore now no condemnation to them which are in
Christ Jesus."

ROMANS 8:1, KJV

PG. 283

A B C D E F G H I J K L M N O P Q R S T
U V W X Y Z

" BUT   WHEN   THE
TIME   HAD   FULLY
COME   ,   GOD   SENT
HIS   SON   ,   BORN   OF
A   WOMAN   ,   BORN
UNDER   LAW   ,   TO
REDEEM   THOSE
UNDER   LAW   ,   THAT
WE   MIGHT   RECEIVE
THE   FULL   RIGHTS
OF   SONS   ."

GALATIANS 4:4–5

1. H E A R T (S)
2. C A (L) L S
3. S T (A) N D
4. R E C E I (V) E
5. F R (E) E
6. S P (I) R I T
7. F U L L (Y)

"IT IS FOR FREEDOM THAT CHRIST HAS SET US FREE. STAND FIRM, THEN, AND DO NOT LET YOURSELVES BE BURDENED AGAIN BY A YOKE OF S L A V E R Y."

GALATIANS 5:1

ASK YOURSELF
ANSWERS

1. THE CURSE OF THE LAW.

2. HE BECAME A CURSE FOR US.

3. HE WAS "HUNG ON A TREE."

4. THE PROMISE OF THE SPIRIT.

5. NO.

6. THE LAW OF SIN AND DEATH.

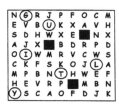

"For the person who keeps all of the laws except one is as g u i l t y as a person who has broken all of God's laws.'

JAMES 2:10, NLT

1. F A (C) E
2. F (U) L L N E S S
3. (R) E L Y
4. K E E P (S)
5. W R I T T (E) N
6. S T A N (D)

"ALL WHO RELY ON OBSERVING THE LAW ARE UNDER A CURSE, FOR IT IS WRITTEN: 'C U R S E D IS EVERYONE WHO DOES NOT CONTINUE TO DO EVERYTHING WRITTEN IN THE BOOK OF THE LAW.'"

GALATIANS 3:10

1. PEOPLE   MURDER
   SUBJECT
2. ANYONE   SANHEDRIN
   DANGER

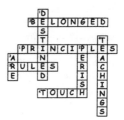

"Woe unto you, scribes and Pharisees, hypocrites! for ye make clean the outside of the cup and of the platter, but within they are full of extortion and excess."

MATTHEW 23:25, KJV

PG. 300–301

ASK YOURSELF
ANSWERS

1. JUST ONE PART.

2. THE WHOLE LAW.

3. SIN.

4. THE POWER OF SIN IS THE LAW.

5. NO.

6. TO CHRIST.

PG. 305

A B C D E F G H I J K L M N O P Q R S T U V W X Y Z

" FOR IF THERE HAD BEEN NOTHING WRONG WITH THAT FIRST COVENANT , NO PLACE WOULD HAVE BEEN SOUGHT FOR ANOTHER BUT GOD FOUND FAULT WITH THE PEOPLE ."

HEBREWS 8:7–8

PG. 307

" WE KNOW THAT THE LAW IS SPIRITUAL ; BUT I AM UNSPIRITUAL , SOLD AS A SLAVE TO SIN . I DO NOT UNDERSTAND WHAT I DO . FOR WHAT I WANT TO DO I DO NOT DO , BUT WHAT I HATE I DO . AND IF I DO WHAT I DO NOT WANT TO DO , I AGREE THAT THE LAW IS GOOD . AS IT IS , IT IS NO LONGER I MYSELF WHO DO IT , BUT IT IS SIN LIVING IN ME ."

ROMANS 7:14–17

376

"I HAVE BEEN <u>C R U C I F I E D</u>
13 34 37 13 22 16 22 15 14

WITH <u>C H R I S T</u> AND I NO
13 21 34 22 35 36

<u>L O N G E R</u> LIVE, BUT CHRIST
25 31 27 17 15 34

<u>L I V E S</u> IN ME. THE LIFE I
25 22 41 15 35

<u>L I V E</u> IN THE <u>B O D Y</u> I
25 22 41 15   12 31 14 44

LIVE BY <u>F A I T H</u> IN THE
16 11 22 36 21

<u>S O N</u> OF GOD, WHO <u>L O V E D</u>
35 31 27   25 31 41 15 14

ME AND GAVE <u>H I M S E L F</u>
21 22 26 35 15 25 16

FOR ME."

GALATIANS 2:20

ASK YOURSELF
ANSWERS

1. NO.

2. NO.

3. WHAT WE DO NOT WANT TO DO.

4. THIRTY-SEVEN TIMES.

5. ME, MYSELF, AND I.

6. CHRIST LIVES IN US.

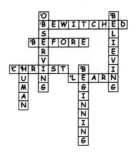

"I am <u>shocked</u> that you are turning <u>away</u> so soon from <u>God</u>, who called you to himself through the loving <u>mercy</u> of Christ. You are <u>following</u> a different way that <u>pretends</u> to be the <u>Good</u> News but is not the Good <u>News</u> at all. You are being <u>fooled</u> by those who deliberately <u>twist</u> the truth concerning Christ."

GALATIANS 1:6-7, NLT

```
F Z H C I N M E J
M B Q L V A T G P
W U G P J V D U B
C E I F U B V F Z
Z V A N D Q N O T
I D L R T G U H M
G P J N K I C P A
Q Z T H B F E J L
A E L D Q M S H C
```

"And if by grace, then is it no more of <u>w o r k s</u>: otherwise grace is no more grace."

ROMANS 11:6, KJV

ASK YOURSELF
ANSWERS

1. BY GRACE ALONE!

2. GRACE COULD NOT BE GRACE.

3. NO VALUE AT ALL.

4. LET'S HOPE NOT!

5. TO LEAD US TO CHRIST.

6. IN YOU.

"THEREFORE, SINCE WE
HAVE BEEN JUSTIFIED
THROUGH FAITH, WE HAVE

PEACE WITH GOD THROUGH
OUR LORD JESUS CHRIST,
THROUGH WHOM WE HAVE

GAINED ACCESS
BY FAITH INTO THIS GRACE
IN WHICH WE NOW STAND. AND WE

REJOICE IN THE
HOPE OF THE GLORY
OF GOD."

ROMANS 5:1-2

GRACE   BEEN
SAVED   FAITH
YOURSELVES   GIFT
WORKS   BOAST

A B C D E F G H I J K L M N O P Q R S T
U V W X Y Z

" BUT   BECAUSE   OF
HIS   GREAT   LOVE
FOR   US   GOD   WHO
IS   RICH   IN   MERCY
MADE   US   ALIVE
WITH   CHRIST   EVEN
WHEN   WE   WERE   DEAD
IN   TRANSGRESSIONS
- IT   IS   BY   GRACE
YOU   HAVE   BEEN
SAVED ."

EPHESIANS 2:4-5

" IN   HIM   WE   HAVE
REDEMPTION   THROUGH
HIS   BLOOD .   THE
FORGIVENESS   OF   SINS
IN   ACCORDANCE
WITH   THE   RICHES
OF   GOD'S   GRACE
THAT   HE   LAVISHED
ON   US   WITH
ALL   WISDOM   AND
UNDERSTANDING ."

EPHESIANS 1:7-8

Crossword (PG. 333):

```
W   R
A P P E A R E D
S   N
H   N
I   E   G
N  S A V E D
G   L   E
C       N
H       E
R I G H T E O U S
I       U
S       S
T       L
    M E R C Y
```

PG. 335:

1. O F F E R E D
2. R E G A R D
3. B R I E F L Y
4. T R U E
5. T H I N G S
6. G I F T
7. F U L L
8. E T E R N A L

"WITH THE HELP OF SILAS, WHOM I REGARD AS A F A I T H F U L BROTHER, I HAVE WRITTEN TO YOU BRIEFLY, ENCOURAGING YOU."

1 PETER 5:12

PG. 336–337

ASK YOURSELF
ANSWERS

1. PEACE WITH GOD.

2. GRACE.

3. IT IS A GIFT OF GOD.

4. NO!

5. MADE US ALIVE WITH CHRIST.

6. BECAUSE OF HIS GREAT LOVE FOR US.

If you enjoyed
Super Bible Activities for Kids 2,
check out these other books
from Barbour Publishing!

Super Bible Word Games for Kids
ISBN 978-1-60260-392-9

Super Bible Crosswords for Kids
ISBN 978-1-60260-474-2

Super Clean Jokes for Kids
ISBN 978-1-60260-391-2

384 pages of fun in each book. . .for only $5.97!

Available wherever Christian books are sold.